Avoiding Workplace Discrimination:
A Guide for Employers and Employees

Avoiding Workplace Discrimination:
A Guide for Employers and Employees

David Harris

Self-Counsel Press
(a division of)
International Self-Counsel Press Ltd.
USA   Canada

Self-Counsel Press acknowledges the financial support of the Government of Canada through the Canada Book Fund for our publishing activities.

Printed in Canada.

First edition: 2015

Library and Archives Canada Cataloguing in Publication

Harris, David, 1949-, author
  Avoiding workplace discrimination : a guide for employers and employees / David Harris.

Issued in print and electronic formats.
ISBN 978-1-77040-214-0 (pbk.).—ISBN 978-1-77040-972-9 (epub).—ISBN 978-1-77040-973-6 (kindle)

  1. Discrimination in employment—Law and legislation—Canada. I. Title.

KE3254.H36 2014	344.7101'133	C2014-905626-5
		C2014-905627-3
KF3464.H36 2014		

Self-Counsel Press
(a division of)
International Self-Counsel Press Ltd.

Bellingham, WA	North Vancouver, BC
USA	Canada

Contents

7 Reinstatement Remedies

8 Duty to Mitigate Income Loss

Notice to Readers

Laws are constantly changing. Every effort is made to keep this publication as current as possible. However, the author, the publisher, and the vendor of this book make no representations or warranties regarding the outcome or the use to which the information in this book is put and are not assuming any liability for any claims, losses, or damages arising out of the use of this book. The reader should not rely on the author or the publisher of this book for any professional advice. Please be sure that you have the most recent edition.

Website links often expire or web pages move, at the time of this book's publication the links were current.

Introduction

All human rights cases must find the origin of the case in the relevant human rights statute. Each jurisdiction in Canada has a statute setting out the definition of what human rights are protected and how the case may be pursued. You should focus on precedent cases from within your own jurisdiction if possible and, if not, then use precedent cases from other jurisdictions.

You should be aware of the dramatic remedies available under human rights law. The following cases are vivid examples of the powerful nature of the remedy available in this manner:

- *A woman in Calgary, a victim of sexual harassment, recovered more than $800,000 in her claim against her employer, in the City of Calgary v. CUPE Local 38, 2013.[1]*

- *A 2012 decision in Alberta, Walsh v. Mobil Oil,[2] allowed for a total damage award of $656,920 because of adverse treatment due to gender and retaliation.*

- *In a 2013 case against the City of Hamilton,[3] an award was made by the Ontario Human Rights Tribunal of eight years back pay of*

1 *City of Calgary v. CUPE Local 38,* accessed September 2014.
   http://www.canlii.org/en/ab/abgaa/doc/2013/2013canlii88297/2013canlii88297.html
2 *Walsh v. Mobil Oil,* accessed September 2014.
   http://www.canlii.org/en/ab/abqb/doc/2012/2012abqb527/2012abqb527.html
3 *Sharon Fair v. Hamilton-Wentworth District School Board,* accessed September 2014.
   http://www.canlii.org/en/on/onhrt/doc/2013/2013hrto440/2013hrto440.html?searchUrlHash=
   AAAAAQAbY2loeSBoYW1pbHRvbiByZWluc3RhdGVtZW50AAAAAAE

*$420,000 plus reinstatement due to the employer's failure to ac-
commodate the applicant's disability by allowing for a return to
work following her disability. The sum of $30,000 was awarded
to compensate for the applicant's injured feelings. The time clock
for the lost income claim continues to tick pending the appeal made
by the employer.*

- *An award of a potential ten-year income loss was made in 2001
by the Canadian Human Rights Tribunal due to discrimination on
account of gender in McAvinn v. Strait Crossing Bridge Ltd.[4]*

The Federal Court of Appeal has recently confirmed that "family status" protections of human rights codes also cover child-care responsibilities.

Most cases referenced in this publication include links in the footnotes
to the full text of the decision which is a free public service database available at www.canlii.ca.

Some of the earlier cases are not available electronically. They are usually reported as Canadian Human Rights Reporter (CHRR) with a volume
and page number. These cases are not available anywhere on the Internet
apart from buying an expensive subscription. The reporting series can be
found at most law libraries at the local courthouse where you will regret-
tably need to either borrow the reporting service or photocopy or scan the
case.

If there is an unreported case you wish to use, enter the name of the
case in the search function of the public service database and you will
likely find other decisions which reference it, which you can then use at a
hearing.

---

4   *McAvinn v. Strait Crossing Bridge Ltd.*, accessed September 2014.
    http://www.canlii.org/en/ca/chrt/doc/2001/2001canlii7954/2001canlii7954.html

1

Human Rights Claims v. Wrongful Dismissal Cases

Human rights remedies are very different and much more powerful than the usual employment law cases that are brought in civil court by an employee. To understand the differences, we should first take a look at what the basic employment law remedies offer, as distinct from a human rights complaint. Then we can understand the differences and why, for the most part, a human rights case has far more impact.

We need to keep in mind a very simple concept: Not every case of unfair treatment or termination in the workplace leads to a human rights complaint. There are many cases in which a person can be treated very unfairly at work, even abusively, but there will be no human rights case possible. To succeed in a human rights complaint, there must be conduct of the employer which is in violation of the relevant human rights code of your provincial, territorial, or federal jurisdiction.

1. Wrongful Dismissal

Wrongful dismissal (also known as wrongful termination or wrongful discharge) is considered a breach of the employment contract. Some of the areas that can cause a wrongful dismissal include discrimination, retaliation, an employee's refusal to commit an illegal act, and the employer not following the company's own termination procedure.

Let's discuss what are considered the "normal" claims an employee can make when terminated, where there is no human rights complaint raised. In a typical employment law civil case, the trigger point will be a termination of employment.

The usual employment law principles require payment or notice to be provided to a person who has been terminated:

Statutory severance pay: This is a minimum payment or, alternatively, working notice, which must be given by an employer to an employee on termination of employment without cause. This sum is set by the relevant provincial, territorial, or federal statute and typically is quite modest. In Ontario, for example, the notice period after three months of employment, is one week and continues as a week per year up to eight weeks maximum. Ontario's statutory payments, unlike other jurisdictions, become comparatively generous, once the payroll exceeds $2.5 million annually for persons employed for more than five years.

Common-law wrongful dismissal claim: Presuming that there is no written contract of employment, the common law or judge-made law, will require the employer to provide advance working notice or, in its absence, the employee can claim his or her earnings that would have been earned in this notice period. This is commonly called a "wrongful dismissal" action.

The amount of notice will be shaped by the individual circumstances in question. The notice period may be as short as the statutory minimum, which is unusual, or as long as two years, for a long-term senior executive.

The statutory severance will reduce the common-law claim, as will any alternate income earned in this notice period. To enforce the common-law claim, the employee must start a case in a civil court. The employer may defend the claim based on an argument of just cause. Suffice it to say in this brief summary, that cause is difficult to prove.

If there is an employment contract which defines the severance sum or notice to be provided to the employee, this will define the claim by employment law concepts on termination.

A human rights case will be able to be pursued without regard to the limiting features of the employment contract, even if the agreement is silent on human rights issues. For example, a contract which allows the company to terminate the employee without cause on the payment of six months' salary, this six-month clause will not be a limiting defence to a claim for compensation under a human rights claim.

2. Human Rights Violation

A human rights violation includes discrimination based on sex, gender, age, national origin, sexual orientation, religion, marital and family status, pardoned criminal convictions, and medical handicaps (or conditions). The Act also specifies that women and men should receive equal pay for work that is of equal value. Human rights cases most often fall into two broad categories: sexual harassment and discrimination.

2.1 Remedy by proof

Let's presume that you can make a claim for a human rights violation. You then need to determine the type of remedy which you may be awarded by the human rights tribunal.

There are three basic types of relief that may be ordered as direct compensation to you as the complainant:

- *Damages for injured feelings.*

- *Lost income, past and occasionally future.*

- *Reinstatement.*

There may also be a public interest award, which is not directed to you personally, but rather directed to the common interests of society and other employees of the company. The important points to note for the present moment are the following:

- *Your claim for income loss is not determined based on wrongful dismissal employment law concepts, but rather on the principle of "make whole," which is usually more generous. (See Chapter 7 for more information.)*

- *You may be awarded reinstatement, a remedy which is foreign to wrongful dismissal actions, and one which is very powerful.*

- *Your claim for reinstatement can be used to support a claim for lost income to the date of the hearing and when refused, can also be used to support your argument for a prospective income loss beyond the date of the final decision (as was the case in the sexual harassment claim against the City of Calgary, which is mentioned in the Introduction).*

Apart from a direct award to the complainant, there can also be a public interest remedy, such as a requirement to post human rights literature in the workplace, mandatory human rights training for the employer, or orders of a similar remedial nature.

In some jurisdictions, such as Ontario, if a company does business with the government but commits a human rights violation, the company will be in breach of its contract. This will allow the government to terminate that contract without compensation to the wrongdoer. This can be a tremendous risk to an employer and also gives a lot of incentive to the company to settle the case privately without a public hearing. Settlements typically have a confidentiality provision which means you cannot reveal the terms of resolution. Also, lawyers always include a term which says that the fact of the settlement is not a legal admission of wrongdoing by the company. This provides a strong impetus to an employer with a government contract in hand to settle the case.

2.2 Remedy without proof

You can bring the following types of human rights claims and recover financial compensation even though the main human rights complaint may fail:

Failure to investigate: The employer has an obligation to take reasonable steps to review the alleged offensive behaviour and determine the merits of the claim. In Ontario, the failure to do so will result in an award of financial compensation in favour of the complainant, even if your substantive claim of a human rights violation fails.

Reprisal: Similarly, should the company treat you adversely due to your decision to file a complaint, a remedy may follow, even where you do not succeed in the main complaint of unfair human rights treatment. Where the reprisal involved a termination, you may claim relief for injured feelings, lost income, and reinstatement.

The statute recognizes that it is inherently unfair for an employer to retaliate against you for exercising your protected legal rights as long as you are doing so in good faith and not inventing a fake case.

Failure to co-operate in the investigation: In certain jurisdictions, such as BC and Nunavut, the statute allows for a costs order to deter improper conduct. Nunavut allows such an order to be made against a party which attempts to impede the investigatory process, which is also independent of the success on the main issue.

2
Employment Relationship and Location of the Incident

This chapter will help you understand what the differences are between self-employment and contracted work. Another consideration is whether or not the incident qualifies as a human rights code violation when the situation occurs outside the workplace.

1. Are You Considered a Self-Employed Contractor or an Employee?

To show jurisdiction of the human rights code, you must be able to show an employment relationship, which is a requirement of all human rights statutes. Human rights laws offer many forms of protection such as housing and public services, but what we are looking at here are only employment-related human rights issues. The great majority of human rights cases are employment related.

There is no definition of "employment" in the human rights codes in Canada so the tribunals have interpreted the term for the purposes of human rights law. Some jurisdictions do state in the statute what the term includes, as opposed to offering a concrete definition. You will see the basic impact of the interpretation given by the precedent cases is that there has developed a very liberal assessment of what qualifies for an employment relationship.

You should also be aware that other determinations of self-employment or independent contractor status for other legal purposes such as income tax, or employment insurance, have been determined to be of no consequence to the human rights tribunal.

Some statutes may offer a statement which allow for a mandatory inclusion of certain relationships, such as personal service contracts. My view is that this provision does not conclusively define employment but rather states what must be included in the word's meaning.

The *Canadian Human Rights Act* contains such a provision, which states that "employment" includes a contractual relationship by which an individual provides services personally.

The federal legislation applies only to federally regulated industries such as banking, telecommunications, radio and television stations, cable businesses, interprovincial transportation businesses, port authorities, railroads, First Nations businesses, federal Crown corporations, and similarly situated businesses. The fact that a company may be incorporated under federal law, as opposed to provincial, does not mean that it is covered by federal law.

The following defines the provincial and territorial definitions of employment or contract workers:

- *The British Columbia statute does not define "employment" exclusively by its terms, but states that it includes principal and agent, where a substantial part of the agent's services relates to the affairs of the principal.*

- *Alberta defines employees as people who work under an employer-employee contract of service while contractors work under an independent business.*

- *The law of Northwest Territories has a similar term which states that employment includes a contractual relationship for the provision of personal services.*

- *Nunavut's statute contains an inclusionary term which allows for protection to work that is paid or unpaid.*

- *Saskatchewan does not define employment. It does state that the term "employee" includes a person engaged pursuant to a limited term contract.*

- *Manitoba offers no definition of employment, nor does it offer inclusionary terms, as is the case in Quebec, New Brunswick, Newfoundland and Labrador, and Yukon.*

- *Nova Scotia and Prince Edward Island both state that the term "employer" includes a person who contracts with a second person for services to be performed wholly or partly by another person.*

The following cases are from Ontario but there is every expectation that they will be used in other jurisdictions to interpret the concept of employment.

- *Payette v. Alarm Guard Services (Dimovski):[1] The company argued that Ms. Payette was a contractor, not an employee, and for that reason, could not use the remedy under the code.*

- *The Ontario Human Rights Tribunal continued that the distinction between contractor and employee was not relevant with respect to the application of the code, given a "purposive, functional approach to determining the test of employment." The employer's submission accordingly failed.*

- *A similar conclusion was reached in Sutton v. Jarvis Ryan Associates,[2] also a decision of the Ontario Human Rights Tribunal. The complainant used a management corporation through which she billed the respondent, a firm of chartered accountants for her services as a bookkeeper. The company similarly defended the case by arguing that she was not an employee.*

- *The Tribunal noted that human rights statutes must be given a liberal interpretation to allow its remedial intent to receive a full application:*

  - *[95] The Supreme Court of Canada has consistently held that human rights statutes across Canada should be given a fair, large and liberal interpretation to advance and fulfill their purposes of preventing discrimination against identifiable protected groups.*

The Tribunal continued to state that the protections of the Code include more than the traditional employer-employee relationship. This is an important concept which you should note in the event your apparent relationship may not fit neatly into what may be expected in a normal employment relationship. Here are the words of the Tribunal:

- *[97] As the Board of Inquiry stated in Payne v. Otsuka Pharmaceuticals Co Ltd., 2001 CanLII 26231 (ON HRT), 2001 CanLII 26231 (ON H.R.T.)[3]*

Section 5(1) does not state that "no employer shall deny equal treatment to an employee." Indeed, there is no definition of "employment" in the Code. Rather, section 5(1) involves discrimination "with respect to

---

1   *Payette v. Alarm Guard Services (Dimovski)*, accessed September 2014.
    http://www.canlii.org/en/on/onhrt/doc/2011/2011hrto109/2011hrto109.html
2   *Sutton v. Jarvis Ryan Associates*, accessed September 2014.
    http://www.canlii.org/en/on/onhrt/doc/2010/2010hrto2421/2010hrto2421.html
3   *Payne v. Otsuka Pharmaceuticals Co Ltd.*, accessed September 2014.
    http://www.canlii.org/en/on/onhrt/doc/2001/2001canlii26231/2001canlii26231.html

employment." "Equal treatment with respect to employment without discrimination" includes more than the traditional employer-employee relationship. In *Canada (Attorney General) v. Rosin* (1990), 16 C.H.R.R. D/441, the Federal Court of Appeal, in upholding the decision of the Canadian Human Rights Tribunal, stated at D/449:

> Remembering the broad and liberal interpretation that must be taken to this type of legislation ... [C]ourts have interpreted the words [i.e., "employ" and "employment"] broadly, finding employment relationships to exist in this context where in other contexts they might not have so found.

In this particular case, the complainant was dependent on the company for her work assignments, use of the facilities, setting her fee for clients, and the supervision of work done by firm members. The employer's argument that the claimant lacked the status of an employee accordingly failed.

2. Events in the Context of Employment but Happen Outside the Workplace

Apart from showing an employment relationship, you must also show that there is jurisdiction of the human rights board by showing that the alleged offence took place within the context of the employment relationship. For example, if you were sexually harassed by your boss, and that conduct took place outside the work environment, the tribunal must be convinced that the alleged offence was somehow connected to the employment context and not independent of it. You may be able to show that there was a promise of a promotion or a raise made at a restaurant which would be good enough to show an employment connection.

If the accused person was a coworker or held a more senior position in another department and the event took place outside of any employment context, it may be difficult to assert that this was employment related.

If there is no conduct which is part of the employment relationship, there would be no possibility of using the human rights code for a remedy.

There is case law on which you can rely to show that just because something happened outside of the office, due to this fact alone, does not mean that it is not within the employment relationship.

The Ontario Court of Appeal in its 2001 decision of *Simpson v. Consumers Association of Canada*[4] dealt with the issue of conduct which did not take place in the immediate workplace, but rather in locations beyond the physical premises of the office. This was not a human rights complaint but a civil lawsuit brought by Mr. Simpson against his employer. The company defended the case by arguing just cause for dismissal, based on allegations of conduct of sexual harassment committed by Mr. Simpson.

The company's defence at the trial was not successful. The employer appealed successfully and the trial decision was set aside. The claim was

---

4   *Simpson v. Consumers Association of Canada*, accessed September 2014.
    http://www.canlii.org/en/on/onca/doc/2001/2001canlii23994/2001canlii23994.html

dismissed on appeal as the employer had proven just cause for dismissal, based on the conduct of the plaintiff sexually harassing employees of the company.

One of the questions considered by the Court of Appeal was the issue that certain of the alleged misconducts took place at locations external to the office premises. The company accordingly needed to prove that the abusive conduct was connected to the employment relationship, even though the events took place outside of the physical premises of the normal business environment.

Three of the events alleged against the plaintiff took place at company meetings or retreats held at hotels which were business meetings but included a social component. The fact that such events occurred after the completion of business meetings did not mean, the Court determined, that such conduct was outside the workplace and hence external to the employment context.

The Court also considered an event which took place at the plaintiff's cottage. Again, this was seen as work related. Staff had been present at the cottage because the plaintiff was on vacation and his advice was required on certain timely business issues. Following the work assignment, the staff was invited to remain and recreate.

The bigger picture which comes from this decision is that a work relationship is not one confined to the office or business premises, but rather a broad contextual view is taken to determine whether the event was work-related or not. The same test will apply to human rights cases.

A similar issue arose in *Sutton v. Jarvis Ryan Associates*, which was a 2010 human rights case in Ontario, where the alleged offensive conduct took place at a firm retreat in South Carolina. The Ontario Human Rights Tribunal found that there was jurisdiction as the event was again work-related.

The British Columbia Supreme Court came to the same view in *van Woerkens v. Marriott Hotels of Canada Ltd.*,[5] a 2009 decision, in which the questioned behaviour took place at an after-party in a hotel room following the employer's holiday party, in this instance in a hotel owned by the defendant, and attended by employees and spouses.

The Nova Scotia Human Rights Board of Inquiry also found that a barbeque event was similarly sufficiently connected to employment to allow for jurisdiction to be found in the 2005 decision of *Davison v. Nova Scotia Construction Safety Association*.[6]

In 2012, the Ontario Human Rights Tribunal found in *Taylor-Baptiste v. Ontario Public Service Employees Union*[7] that comments made in cyberspace may well fit into the category of workplace communications

---

5 *van Woerkens v. Marriott Hotels of Canada Ltd.*, accessed September 2014.
   http://www.canlii.org/en/bc/bcsc/doc/2009/2009bcsc73/2009bcsc73.html
6 *Davison v. Nova Scotia Construction Safety Association*, accessed September 2014.
   http://www.canlii.org/en/ns/nshrc/doc/2005/2005nshrc4/2005nshrc4.html
7 *Taylor-Baptiste v. Ontario Public Service Employees Union*, accessed September 2014.
   http://www.canlii.org/en/on/onhrt/doc/2012/2012hrto1393/2012hrto1393.html

but in this instance concluded that the communication in question, which was a blog, was intended as a discussion between union members and was not caught by the definition of workplace. For this reason, the complaint could not proceed.

3
Understanding the Process

This chapter will give you a basic understanding of the process and terminology you will need as you proceed with your complaint.

1. The Parties to the Case

The vocabulary used for the parties to the case is usually the "applicant" or "complainant" for the party starting the case. These terms are used interchangeably to refer to the party starting the case in this publication, which may not be technically the correct term in each jurisdiction.

The "respondent" is the company or person who is named in the case as being responsible for the relief sought. You will name the employer in most cases as the respondent. Any apparently related companies that may be involved in the business should also be named.

2. The Process: Direct User Access or Human Rights Commission's Control over the Case

The status of the body known as the Human Rights Commission can be confusing. This arises due to the two different methods by which a complaint can be advanced.

The first is the "direct user access" system which allows an individual to commence a complaint and take the case to hearing on his or her own initiative, with or without legal counsel. Ontario, BC, and Nunavut use this system.

The second process gives the local Human Rights Commission control over the case. In the remaining jurisdictions, the case starts by the complainant contacting the Human Rights Commission, which investigates the allegation and initiates the case, and always with the individual also as a party.

In Ontario, which uses the direct user access process, the Human Rights Commission usually is not a party to the case. It acts as an advisory body to the public. In cases of widescale public interest or involving important legal issues, the Human Rights Commission may seek to add itself as a party to the case. Typically the complainant is shown as the only party initiating the case. Where the Commission has been added as a party, the complainant is a distinct and separate party at the hearing before the tribunal. He or she has the right to participate and may take positions that are different from those expressed by the Commission.

If you believe that your case fits into the possible ambit of a case of interest to the Ontario Human Rights Commission, you should direct your inquiry to the Commission.[1] The big advantage to you is that benefit from the considerable resources, experience, and muscle of the Commission and likely, if your respective interests are harmonious, you need not incur the expense of your own legal counsel or at least your own counsel throughout the process.

Only British Columbia and Nunavut do not have a body known as a human rights commission. The court, or tribunal more appropriately, which hears the case is referred to as a human rights panel, board, board of inquiry, or tribunal. It is this body which is the decision maker in the case.

In Alberta, the complainant is a party, as also is the Director of the Human Rights Commission in every case. Saskatchewan follows the same process as does Manitoba, New Brunswick, Nova Scotia, Prince Edward Island, and Newfoundland and Labrador.

Quebec's Charter of Human Rights and Freedoms allows the Commission to have carriage of the case. Should it decide not to pursue the claim, the individual may continue the case on his or her initiative.

The statute of the Yukon is a hybrid, incorporating elements of both systems. The user files the complaint and the Human Rights Commission then investigates the merits of the action. The Commission may advocate the position of either adverse party at the hearing before the panel, which is a sensible approach.

The law of the Northwest Territories permits the complainant to commence the complaint or the Commission, in which the latter case it is a

1   Ontario Human Rights Commission, accessed September 2014.
    http://www.ohrc.on.ca/en/about-commission

party. The Commission may also advise the panel in which event it is also a party.

2.1 Power of the commissions

In systems which do not allow for a direct user access process, the Commission retains the power to determine if a particular case should proceed to hearing. The specific legislative provisions vary, but the substance is similar. Generally speaking, if the Commission feels that the case is without merit, or the complainant has remedies in other forums such as a union grievance, the Commission can order the case to be dismissed and no hearing will be held.

Some statutes state that if the Commission feels a reasonable offer from the employer is presented, and the complainant will not accept it, the Commission has the power to refuse to submit the case to hearing and dismiss the matter. This is the law in Alberta, Saskatchewan, Manitoba, Yukon, and Prince Edward Island.

Quebec's Charter allows for the individual to continue the case where the Commission elects not to proceed. The law of the Northwest Territories allows for the employee to appeal the decision of the Commission to dismiss the case, as does that of New Brunswick. Although the right of the review of such a decision of the Commission to dismiss the case is not specifically set out in other statutes, there can be doubt that this is a statutory decision entitling the employee to seek a review of such decision in a higher court.

Effectively, this means that the Commission is the gatekeeper, controlling the process by which cases proceed to hearing. The direct user access systems allow for pre-hearing motions by which the employer argues, in similar terms, that the case is without merit and should be dismissed without a full hearing.

3. Class Actions

The legislations of BC, Northwest Territories, and Nunavut allow for a group action to be commenced. This is a very valuable tool which dramatically adds to the punch of the claim and negotiating clout. It is odd that other jurisdictions have not allowed for this process, as quite often a systemic rule or practice implemented by an employer may have consequences for many people.

The potential power in the use of this process is reflected in the Human Rights Tribunal decision in *Balikawa obo others v. Khaira Enterprises and others*.[2] The 55 complainants each recovered $10,000 for compensatory damages for injured dignity and self-respect in a case based on unfair treatment due to race plus a lost income claim of up to three months at $1,000 a month each.

---

2 *Balikawa obo others v. Khaira Enterprises and others*, accessed September 2014.
http://www.canlii.org/en/bc/bchrt/doc/2014/2014bchrt107/2014bchrt107.html

4. Vicarious Liability

The principle of "vicarious liability" means that the employer is legally responsible for the acts of its employees which take place in the course of employment. Most human rights statutes deem that the company is responsible for the actions of its employees, officers, and directors in that circumstance.

There is also a well-known decision in the Supreme Court of Canada which came to the same conclusion in a circumstance where there did not exist such a "deeming" provision imposing liability on the employer by the relevant human rights statute. Accordingly, there are two arguments for finding that the employer is responsible for the acts of its employees: the statutory provision; and where there is none, the Supreme Court of Canada decision of *Robichaud v. Canada (Treasury Board)*.[3]

Generally speaking, for this reason, apart from the exceptions, and presuming that the company is financially solvent, there is no need to name any individuals personally as respondents.

There are some important exceptions to vicarious liability. Many jurisdictions by the relevant legislation have amended the concept by which an employer has been determined to be responsible for the actions of its employees, as described below:

- *Ontario's legislation by section 46.3 (1) creates a deeming provision holding an employer responsible for the conduct of its officer, official, employee, or agent in the course of his or her employment. This provision does not apply to certain claims. These are Section 5(2) freedom from harassment in the workplace, Section 7 sexual harassment in the workplace and sexual solicitation and freedom from reprisal connected to sexual solicitation.*

  - *You must note that there is no deemed liability on the employer for wrongdoings under these remedy sections under the Ontario Code. Thus, under the Ontario Code, the deeming provision holding the employer responsible for the acts of its employees, agents, or officers, does not apply to sexual harassment. Those complaints must be brought personally against the individual who is accused of the offensive conduct. If you are claiming sexual harassment, be sure to name the alleged wrongdoers personally. This is very important.*

The Ontario Human Rights Tribunal publishes a guide for the filing of human rights complaints, which discourages employees from naming personal respondents. This should be ignored in sexual harassment cases.

- *BC does not have such a "deeming provision" as in the case of Ontario. Accordingly the relevant law is as set out in the Supreme Court of Canada 1987 decision in Robichaud v. Canada (Treasury Board) [1987] 2 SCR 84, which concluded that the employer should*

---

3   *Robichaud v. Canada (Treasury Board)*, accessed September 2014.
    http://www.canlii.org/en/ca/scc/doc/1987/1987canlii73/1987canlii73.html

be responsible, in a human rights context, for all acts of its employ-ees committed in the course of the employment relationship.

- *The BC law is the same as Alberta, Saskatchewan, Nova Sco-tia, Prince Edward Island, Newfoundland and Labrador, Northwest Territories, Nunavut, and Quebec.*

- *Manitoba has enacted legislation which defines the concept of employer liability for the acts of its employees. Provided that the conduct was in the course of employment, the employer is deemed responsible. The employer may show a defence by proving it did not consent to the conduct, took all reasonable steps to prevent it, and then took all reasonable steps to minimize or avoid the effect of the offensive actions.*

The substance of Manitoba's provision is repeated in the legislation of the Yukon.

- *New Brunswick has similar legislation with respect to a complaint of sexual harassment, which deems the actions of the employee to be those of the employer, and then allows the employer a defence of showing it used due diligence to prevent such conduct. This de-fence is not available where the questioned conduct is that of an officer or a director of the employer, which basically incorporates the "organic theory" of employer liability described in section 5. There is no general deeming provision which means the Supreme Court of Canada case will determine employer liability for the ac-tions of its employees, in cases other than sexual harassment.*

Essentially the federal legislation now allows for a "due diligence" de-fence to be raised against the assertion of vicarious liability allowed by section 65(1) and (2).[4] The employer must show that it did not consent to the questioned conduct, it used all due diligence to prevent the event, and did all it could to minimize or avoid the adverse consequences.

4.1 Reprisal and vicarious liability

The Ontario Code contains two sections on the subject of reprisal. The first section is exempt from the deeming provision holding the employer vicari-ously liable for the conduct of its employees or officers, as noted above. The second section is not.

Section 7(3) deals with the right of the employee to be free from sexual solicitation and also contains a prohibition against a reprisal for the rejec-tion of same. This provision is exempted from the deeming provisions of employer liability by section 46.3(1). Section 7(3) reads as follows:

(3) Every person has a right to be free from,

   (a) a sexual solicitation or advance made by a person in a posi-tion to confer, grant or deny a benefit or advancement to the

---

4   *Canadian Human Rights Act,* sections 65(1) and (2), accessed September 2014.
    http://laws-lois.justice.gc.ca/eng/acts/H-6/page-24.html#h-19

person where the person making the solicitation or advance knows or ought reasonably to know that it is unwelcome; or

(b) *a reprisal or a threat of reprisal for the rejection of a sexual solicitation or advance where the reprisal is made or threatened by a person in a position to confer, grant or deny a benefit or advancement to the person. R.S.O. 1990, c. H.19, s. 7 (3).*

For this reason, you must name the employee responsible for the conduct as a personal respondent or the employer must be held responsible by arguing the organic theory of liability as set out below (see section **5.**).

Section 8 of the Ontario Code is the general reprisal section which is not exempted from the deeming provision. The distinction apparently is that section 8 deals with the direct or indirect threat of, or actual commencement of, a claim under the Code; whereas section 7 is the rejection of a sexual solicitation and consequential adverse treatment without the threat of a Code proceeding. Section 8 reads as follows:

Reprisals

8. *Every person has a right to claim and enforce his or her rights under this Act, to institute and participate in proceedings under this Act and to refuse to infringe a right of another person under this Act, without reprisal or threat of reprisal for so doing. R.S.O. 1990, c. H.19, s. 8.*

The distinction is more than subtle, yet very important.

If you are the victim of adverse conduct due to the threat of filing a complaint or the actual filing of a complaint, the employer is legally responsible for this separate part of your claim. This claim may succeed where reprisal or retaliation is proven, even if the main allegation of a human rights violation may fail. For example, if you are fired because the company thinks you are about to file, or you have filed, a human rights complaint for gender bias, you can sue for all the normal types of relief on a reprisal claim. Even if you are unable to prove that you were adversely treated due to gender, your claim may still succeed for damages, lost income, and reinstatement due to the reprisal claim.

5. Organic Theory of Employer Liability

The organic theory of employer liability is a concept that is based on the theory that the employer company is responsible for the conduct of its principals. It is different from vicarious liability. This means that a legal entity can only act through its principals and, hence, the company will be held liable for such conduct in a sexual harassment case, or a similar situation where the statute's deeming provision of liability on the employer does not apply. You can use this argument when the offensive conduct has been committed by the "directing mind" of the company to then hold the employer responsible.

Accordingly, a company may still be held liable with the offenders personally for a sexual harassment claim where the offensive conduct was committed by "the principals" or the "directing mind" of the company.

You should name the directing minds personally and also the company as respondents and then assert that the company is legally responsible for the actions of its top brass. This is essentially what New Brunswick codified in its legislation.

The Ontario Divisional Court considered in 2012 the liability of the personal respondents in *Ontario Human Rights Commission v. Farris*,[5] which was a case of gender discrimination. In this case, the Divisional Court held that the conduct of those persons who may be seen to be the "directing mind" of the corporation will cause resultant liability on both themselves and the corporation. It was an important issue in this case as the company was apparently insolvent.

The directing minds of the corporation were also held personally responsible for the conduct of the company in *deSousa v. Gauthier*,[6] in an Ontario Human Rights Tribunal decision.

5.1 Employer deemed responsible for duty to investigate (Ontario)

You should be aware that Section 5(1) of the Ontario Code also creates an obligation of the corporation to make a proper and timely investigation of the complaint. The resulting liability accordingly is one for which the employer is deemed to be vicariously liable or responsible by virtue of the legislation.

You may be entitled to a damage award for the employer's failure to investigate in Ontario. This may be awarded to you, even where the main claim of the human rights violation fails.

6. The Union As a Respondent

The leading case on the liability of the union in a human rights complaint is the Supreme Court of Canada decision in *Central Okanagan School District No. 23 v. Renaud*,[7] which was decided in September of 1992. The complainant, a Seventh-day Adventist, was employed by the school board as a unionized janitor. The collective agreement required him to work Friday evening, which conflicted with his religious requirements, as the Sabbath commenced at this time.

The board offered a Sunday to Thursday shift to accommodate the religious beliefs of the complainant, but the union refused to accede to this variation of the collective agreement. This resulted in the board's decision

---

5 *Ontario Human Rights Commission v. Farris*, accessed September 2014.
   http://www.canlii.org/en/on/onscdc/doc/2012/2012onsc3876/2012onsc3876.html
6 *deSousa v. Gauthier*, accessed September 2014.
   http://www.canlii.org/en/on/onhrt/doc/2002/2002canlii46506/2002canlii46506.html
7 *Central Okanagan School District No. 23 v. Renaud*, accessed September 2014.
   http://www.canlii.org/en/ca/scc/doc/1992/1992canlii81/1992canlii81.html

to terminate the complainant's employment, hence giving rise to the human rights complaint against the employer and the union.

The Supreme Court determined that the union, which acknowledged that it was under a duty to accommodate, may be a party to discrimination in two ways. The first is a situation where the union has participated in the work rule that has the discriminatory effect on the complainant. Alternatively, the union may be liable even if it did not participate in the creation of such a rule, where it impedes the reasonable efforts of the employer to accommodate.

The union's obligation will differ, as the Court determined, from that of the employer as its duty must be considered in the context of its obligations to other employees which it represents. "Any significant interference with the rights of others" would ordinarily justify the union from refusing to consent to a step of such consequence. The test of undue hardship must be revised to reflect this broad perspective.

In the context of this case, involving the second test, the Court stated the union's duty will arise when no other reasonable alternative resolution could have been reasonably found. In this instance, liability was found on the union and the decision of the human rights board was restored.

The Alberta Court of Appeal in its 2003 decision of *United Food and Commercial Workers, Local 401 v. Alberta Human Rights and Citizenship Commission*[8] considered an appeal from a Human Rights panel decision which had held the employer and the union both responsible for the implementation of a buyout provision which adversely treated disabled employees. This decision had been upheld on a first review before the Queen's Bench of Alberta.

The employer and the union had entered into an agreement by which more senior higher paid employees were offered a buyout of their employments in exchange for which a sum of money was paid and an offer was extended of a lower paying position. The purpose of this plan was to implement a dramatic cost-saving plan, without which the company faced serious financial issues. Disabled employees did not qualify for the buyout, resulting in the human rights complaint.

The Court of Appeal determined that for the purposes of the analysis to determine if there was discrimination, "the comparator group" to be used was the group of employees who were of the same seniority as those offered the buyout. As within this group, the disabled employees were adversely treated, the test of *prima facie* discrimination was met. As to the role of the union, the Court of Appeal agreed with the finding that it had failed in its duty to accommodate to the point of undue hardship.

---

8   *United Food and Commercial Workers, Local 401 v. Alberta Human Rights and Citizenship Commission*, accessed September 2014. http://www.canlii.org/en/ab/abca/doc/2003/2003abca246/2003abca246.html

The Ontario Tribunal decision in *Bubb-Clarke v. Toronto Transit Commission,*[9] a 2002 decision, examined the second branch of the *Renaud* decision.

The applicant was transferred from one division to another division due to a medical condition which necessitated this move. The collective agreement did not allow for a continuity of seniority. Subsequently a lay off was implemented, which was based on years of service, which brought the issue to a head. The employer supported the applicant's request that his entire history of employment be credited, a position to which the union did not accede. To do so, the employer was required to waive a term of the collective agreement. The union was found to be in violation of its duty to accommodate the employee.

In section 6 of the Ontario code, a union may be found to have violated a code obligation should it fail to offer fair representation to a union member due to a prohibited ground of discrimination. This liability is distinct from the section 5 employment liability. The union must not only fail to offer representation but make such decision in a manner which violates the code for liability to follow. Other jurisdictions in Canada offer the same protections.

---

9   *Bubb-Clarke v. Toronto Transit Commission,* accessed September 2014.
    http://www.canlii.org/en/on/onhrt/doc/2002/2002canlii46503/2002canlii46503.html

4
The Grounds of Discrimination

All Canadian jurisdictions ban adverse treatment in an employment context based on race, religion, gender, age, disability, and marital or family status — apart from New Brunswick which offers no family status protection. The precise definition may vary from statute to statute, but the substantive effect is the same.

All jurisdictions offer protection on account of pregnancy, usually as an interpretation of gender. Some specifically define the protected ground as including the perception or possibility of pregnancy and pregnancy-related disabilities, which additional descriptions are included, in any event, in the interpretation of the protected ground.

The interpretation of all human rights protections has been read to capture the perception that the affected person may be included within such a protected right. That is, a company which terminated a person because it believed the person was homosexual would be in violation of the human rights code, even if this perception was mistaken.

The following points discuss certain nuances in individual legislation:

- *The Ontario Code offers as a protected right a record of offences which is a defined term which includes a Criminal Code conviction for which a pardon has been given and any provincial offence.*

- *In Ontario the Code prevents age discrimination for those aged 18 or older.*

- *The rights protected under the BC code include political belief, and a conviction that is unrelated to the employment or to the intended employment of that person.*

- *The Alberta Human Rights Code adds as a protected right "source of income," which is intended to refer to applicants for employment who are on social assistance or similar incomes such as a disability benefit. The intent is to protect those persons in receipt of income sums which attract a social stigma.*

- *Saskatchewan's code similarly offers protection to those persons in receipt of public assistance.*

- *Manitoba's statute offers protection to those persons adversely affected by employment decisions relating to source of income, political belief, association or activity, and uniquely "social disadvantage." The Manitoba Human Rights Commission issued a policy manual interpreting this term to be diminished social standing based on homelessness, low level of education, chronic low income, or chronic unemployment which has led to a negative stereotype.*

- *Quebec's Charter of Human Rights and Freedoms defines the protected rights in employment to include political convictions, language, social conditions (e.g., the situation you have in society due to your level of income or education, or your occupation), and handicap or the use of any means to palliate a handicap. Quebec law also forbids adverse treatment in employment due to a criminal conviction if a pardon has been obtained or the offence is not connected with the employment.*

- *New Brunswick's legislation also extends its mandate to include social condition or political belief or activity.*

- *The statute of Nova Scotia forbids discrimination in employment based on an irrational fear of contracting an illness or a disease, aboriginal origin, source of income, political belief, affiliation, or activity, and that individual's association with another individual or class of individuals having characteristics referred to in the protected rights.*

- *Newfoundland's Human Rights Act adds to its protected human rights social origin, disfigurement, source of income, and political opinion.*

- *The legislation of Prince Edward Island offers its mandate to political belief, source of income, or a person who has been convicted of a criminal or summary conviction offence which is unrelated to the employment of the person or intended employment. The term "political belief" is confined to that of a registered political party.*

- *The Northwest Territories law bans adverse treatment due to family affiliation, political belief, political association, social condition, or a conviction that is subject to a pardon or record suspension.*

- *Nunavut legislation forbids discrimination due to receipt of a lawful source of income, and a conviction for which a pardon has been granted.*

- *The legislation of the Yukon offers protection to those adversely impacted by decisions relating to linguistic background, political belief, association or activity, criminal charges or criminal record, source of income, and actual or presumed association with persons or groups whose identity is determined by a prohibited ground.*

The *Canadian Human Rights Act* provides to its prohibited grounds of discrimination a conviction for an offence for which a pardon has been granted or in respect of which a record suspension has been ordered.

Although the statute of BC does not have a similar provision, the interpretation of "criminal conviction" has been read to include a charge that has, ironically, not resulted in a conviction. For example, as was stated in *Junkin v. BC (Ministry of Attorney General),*[1] a decision of the BC Human Rights Tribunal:

I first consider whether the ground of "criminal conviction" under the Code can extend to criminal behaviour which only led to charges, did not result in conviction and in this case, arguably resulted in the complainant's acquittal.

[21] Past decisions have held that, based on a liberal and purposive interpretation, the ground of "criminal conviction" in s. 13[2] may extend to criminal charges: Dore v. Crown Tire Service Ltd. *(1989), 10 C.H.R.R. D15433 (BC Council of Human Rights). The rationale for extending the protection of the ground of criminal conviction to those charged with a criminal offence, is that it would be inconsistent with a broad application of the Code if an employer could dismiss or otherwise discriminate against a person merely charged with an offence (who might subsequently be proven innocent), but could not do so if that person was convicted. In* Clement v. Jackson and Abdulla, *2006 BCHRT 411, the rationale was extended at para 18:*

In my view, that rationale also extends the ground of criminal conviction to criminal acts which do not result in charges being laid or a conviction registered. It would be an absurd result if Ms. Clement were in a better position with respect to the protections in the Code had she been charged and/or convicted of theft than she is in her current circumstances, where no charges were ever laid. As a result, I conclude that the ground of criminal conviction extends to criminal acts for which no charges were laid as well as to those for which charges were laid but no conviction is registered.

1   *Junkin v. BC (Ministry of Attorney General)*, accessed September 2014.
    http://www.canlii.org/en/bc/bchrt/doc/2011/2011bchrt35/2011bchrt35.html
2   Human Rights Code, section 13, accessed September 2014.
    http://www.canlii.org/en/bc/laws/stat/rsbc-1996-c-210/latest/rsbc-1996-c-210.html#sec13_smooth

One would expect that this broad interpretation would be applied in every jurisdiction. It makes no sense that a person's circumstance would be improved by a conviction and/or subsequent erasure of that record, where the latter is required. Apart from that of the Yukon, the statutes have been poorly drafted and absent such a universal interpretation and should be amended.

1. Types of Human Rights Complaints

Certain types of cases are based on conduct which is overt or obvious. These include cases based on disability, sexual harassment, and family or marital status.

Claims based on other grounds of discrimination such as race, religion, gender, and age tend to be more difficult to prove. Direct evidence in these cases is rare, which is why the standards of proof are more relaxed than in a civil court case.

1.1 Disability cases

The underlying premise dealing with an employee under a disability — whether the issue is termination or a failure to allow a return to active employment following a period of medical absence — is that the employer must show reasonable accommodation to the point of undue hardship.

The employee, to establish a valid claim, must show a *prima facie* (e.g., on first encounter or at first sight) case of discrimination as was considered in *BC (Public Service Agency) v. BC Government and Service Employees Union*.[3] To succeed in this first step, the complainant must show a disability, an apparent adverse treatment by the employer, and a reasonable inference that the disability was a factor in the adverse decision.

You should be very careful to note, that as with all human rights cases, the employee must show only that the adverse treatment was somehow influenced by the disability. You need not prove that the questioned conduct, such as termination of employment, was solely due to the human rights violation.

The employer must then show a defence, just as reasonable accommodation to the point of undue hardship and/or justification or an excepting provision in the relevant statute or a bona fide occupational requirement, which cannot be accommodated.

Many legislatures have defined in the relevant statute what factors may be taken into account to determine "undue hardship." Please take note that the Ontario Code states the factors to be considered in this defence are the cost, outside sources of funding, if any, and health and safety requirements, if any. To succeed in this defence, the employer should introduce its evidence of hardship within these factors.

---

3 BC (Public Service Agency) v. BC Government and Service Employees Union, accessed September 2014.
   http://www.canlii.org/en/bc/bcca/doc/2008/2008bcca357/2008bcca357.html#par6

Once the employer is aware of the general nature of a disability, and given a period of medical absence, it should not terminate without taking reasonable steps to gain information as to the full nature of the medical restrictions and how, if at all, it might accommodate a return to work.

The employee must show that he or she is willing to participate in the accommodation process by sharing whatever information may be required to allow for accommodation.

As to what is the standard of "undue hardship," the test has been developed that some form of hardship is to be expected, given the word "undue." The factors of hardship have been described as an open forum but will include "the financial cost, the relative interchangeability of the workforce and facilities and the prospect of substantial interference with the rights of other employees," as was stated by the *Supreme Court in British Columbia (Public Service Employee Relations Commission) v. BCGSEU* (also known as "Meiorin").[4]

In this case, the Supreme Court developed this test to apply to examine the validity of the employer's bona fide occupational requirement, which in this case was an aerobic standard of fitness which was applied equally to male and female candidates:

1) *it adopted the standard for a purpose or goal that is rationally connected to the function being performed;*

2) *it adopted the standard in good faith, in the belief that it is necessary to the fulfillment of the purpose or goal; and*

3) *that the standard is reasonably necessary to the accomplishment of that legitimate work-related purpose. To show that the standard is reasonably necessary, it must be demonstrated that it is impossible to accommodate individual employees sharing the characteristics of the claimant without imposing undue hardship (including impossibility, serious risk or excessive cost), upon the employer ("Meiorin", para 54) see also British Columbia (Superintendent of Motor Vehicles) v. British Columbia (Council of Human Rights), 1999 CanLII 646 (SCC), [1999] 3 S.C.R. 868 ("Grismer").*[5]

The Supreme Court of Canada in the McGill University Health Centre[6] case considered that in an issue of undue hardship, the factors are not defined, but "must be applied with common sense and flexibility." These will include "the cost of possible accommodation method, employee morale and mobility, the interchangeability of facilities, and the prospect of interference with the other employees' rights or of disruption of the collective agreement."

---

4   *Supreme Court in British Columbia (Public Service Employee Relations Commission) v. BCGSEU* (also known as "Meiorin"), accessed September 2014. http://www.canlii.org/en/ca/scc/doc/1999/ 1999canlii652/1999canlii652.html

5   *British Columbia (Superintendent of Motor Vehicles) v. British Columbia (Council of Human Rights),* accessed September 2014. http://www.canlii.org/en/ca/scc/doc/1999/1999canlii646/1999canlii646.html

6   *McGill University Health Centre (Montreal General Hospital) v. Syndicat des employés de l'Hôpital général de Montréal,* accessed September 2014. http://www.canlii.org/en/ca/scc/doc/2007/2007scc4/ 2007scc4.html

Many legislatures have defined in the relevant statute what factors may be taken into account to determine "undue hardship." The Ontario Code states the factors are the cost, outside sources of funding, if any, and health and safety requirements, if any. To succeed in this defence, the employer should introduce its evidence of hardship within these factors.

The duty to accommodate is not limited to the position held at the time the disability arose. Such was the finding of the *BC Supreme Court in Emergency Health Services Commission v. Cassidy*,[7] a decision made in October of 2010 by Madam Justice Gray, sitting on a judicial review application.

An employee suffering from addiction to drugs or alcohol must accept and pursue treatment to deal with the disability. Presuming that is so, the employer then has an obligation to accommodate up to the point of undue hardship, particularly where the employee has by medical evidence, established that he or she is fit to return to work. Even where the medical evidence may show that there are conditions attached to the return to work, the employer must show whether it can accommodate those conditions without undue hardship.

This principle was reviewed and accepted as a proper statement of law in London Health Sciences Centre[8] in the decision of Arbitrator James Hayes in his January 2013 decision.

1.2 Sexual harassment cases

In 1989, The Supreme Court of Canada in *Janzen v. Platy Enterprises Ltd.*[9] defined sexual harassment in an employment context to be:

Unwelcome conduct of a sexual nature that detrimentally affects the work environment or leads to adverse job-related consequences for the victims of the harassment.

There is an extensive range of conduct which can be found to constitute sexual harassment in human rights cases. It need not be limited to demands for sexual favours. It can be verbal or nonverbal. As was found in *Reed v. Cattolica Investments (McNeilly)* by the Board of Inquiry, as referenced and adopted in *Lavoie v. Calabogie Peaks (Chapman)*,[10] the term covers a broad spectrum:

The following quote describes the wide range of conduct which can be found to constitute sexual harassment within the meaning of the Code:

Sexual harassment need not be only demands made for sexual favours, it can be any type or a single act of overtures, requests, invitations or comments made of a sexual nature, especially when these overtures, requests, invitations or comments are made upon unwilling, vulnerable,

7   *BC Supreme Court in Emergency Health Services Commission v. Cassidy*, accessed September 2014.
    http://www.canlii.org/en/bc/bcsc/doc/2011/2011bcsc1003/2011bcsc1003.html
8   *Ontario Nurses' Association v. London Health Sciences Centre*, accessed September 2014.
    http://www.canlii.org/en/on/onla/doc/2013/2013canlii143/2013canlii143.html
9   *Janzen v. Platy Enterprises Ltd.*, accessed September 2014.
    http://www.canlii.org/en/ca/scc/doc/1989/1989canlii97/1989canlii97.html
10 *Lavoie v. Calabogie Peaks (Chapman)*, accessed September 2014.
    http://www.canlii.org/en/on/onhrt/doc/2012/2012hrto1237/2012hrto1237.html

scared, and job dependent employees by employers, their agents or co-workers. Sexual harassment is a form of sex discrimination, which is clearly prohibited by law. Sexual harassment takes different forms and can occur in different places. Sexual harassment can be any sustained sexual behaviour that a person finds personally offensive. It may be subtle, obvious, verbal or nonverbal. It may be physical or psychological. Sexual harassment can also be effected through the use of profane and abusive language that denigrates a person's gender.

It is clear that one event may give rise to a finding of sexual harassment. A pattern of repeated behaviour is not required. A sexually explicit remark that is clearly demeaning will create a violation.

The offensive remarks in the *Gregory v. Parkbridge Lifestyle Communities Inc. (Jacobs)*[11] were "nice tits" and "how's your love life," both of which were stated on a unique occasion. This conduct was considered to be a violation of the Code. The Tribunal stated in this case:

In appropriate circumstances, a single incident, if serious, will meet the definition of harassment. Repeated conduct is not essential to a finding that the Code has been violated. A sexually explicit remark that is clearly demeaning and attacks the dignity and self-respect of a woman based on her gender will violate the Code … It has long been recognized that sexual harassment is characterized by power imbalance … In the context of accommodation, the jurisprudence indicates that power imbalances between owner and occupant are to be taken into account in cases in which sexual harassment is raised.

A similar finding was made by the *Tribunal in Murchie v. JB's Mongolian Grill (Hendriks)*[12] in which it was found the isolated event was sufficient to warrant a finding of sexual harassment. The complainant had proven that the respondent had "flicked" her nipple.

My review of the case law shows that the definition of what conduct may or may not be actionable sexual harassment becomes contextual based on the legal issue between the parties. A single event of a comparatively minor nature may be actionable as a human rights complaint seeking monetary compensation only or a public interest remedy; yet will likely not support a constructive dismissal allegation or a poisoned work environment in Code vocabulary. That is, the employee could not argue that such conduct "terminated" his or her employment, even though it was a human rights violation.

All this comes from a legal concept that the conduct which is questioned must be serious, fundamental, or "go to the root" of the employment relationship to argue that the relationship was terminated legally. For example, if you ordered a new vehicle and the dealer instead gave you a model which was one year old, you could easily argue that this was a fundamental breach and refuse delivery and payment as the contract was

11 *Gregory v. Parkbridge Lifestyle Communities Inc. (Jacobs)*, accessed September 2014.
   http://www.canlii.org/en/on/onhrt/doc/2011/2011hrto1535/2011hrto1535.html
12 *Tribunal in Murchie v. JB's Mongolian Grill (Hendriks)*, accessed September 2014.
   http://www.canlii.org/en/on/onhrt/doc/2006/2006hrto33/2006hrto33.html#_ftn1

broken. However, if the dealer delivered the new vehicle and failed to install your FM radio, you would need to fulfill your part of the bargain, accept delivery, pay for the vehicle, and then sue for the cost of the new radio. This is a breach of contract, but not one which goes "to the root" of the contract.

The same principles apply in this context of employment and behaviour which may run the gamut of sexually offensive conduct. An example of such a finding is the decision of the Tribunal in *Shroff v. Tipco (Muir)*[13] in which it was determined that the complainant employee suffered abusive behaviour by coworkers who taunted him due to his inability to have a child with his spouse. This conduct was actionable as a complaint under the Code, yet not of sufficient substance to allow for the determination of a poisoned work environment to support in effect, a constructive dismissal:

[11] The Application is allowed in part. The essence of the complaint as framed by Mr. Shroff was that he was forced out of the workplace by a poisoned work environment created by his treatment by the respondent Satesh Shiwkaran. I find for reasons set out below that although Mr. Shroff's Code rights were violated by the respondent Shiwkaran, the conduct did not create a poisoned work environment. I also find that the corporate respondent is responsible for the conduct of Mr. Shiwkaran.

To the same end is the decision of *Watt v. Regional Municipality of Niagara and Wales* (1984) 5 CHRR D/2453 (McCamus) in which the Board concluded that the offensive remarks did not occur with sufficient frequency to create an abusive work environment. The argument that "virtually any insult or joke of an offensive nature which is based on the biological differences between the sexes can constitute an offence under the Code" was rejected as such a conclusion would not be in accordance with "social policy."

For these reasons, you should be cautious about asserting "I've been fired" due to conduct which is sexual harassment. You will need to be sure that you can prove the alleged wrongdoing and that it is serious enough to be considered grounds for such action.

The 1980 decision of the Board of Inquiry, in *Bell v. Ladas* (1980) 1 CHRR D/155 (Shime) was an early case, in fact, the first case to consider a sexual harassment issue in employment in Ontario. The legislation at the time, was the case with the Manitoba statute referenced in *Janzen*, did not then specifically reference sexual harassment to be a violation of the Code and hence the complaint was based on gender. The Board stated that there was a fine line between steps taken to eliminate sexual harassment and conduct which may be considered acceptable social interaction. This led to the famous quotation that "an invitation to dinner is not an invitation to a complaint":

The prohibition against such conduct is not without its dangers. One must be cautious that the law not inhibit normal social contact

---

13 *Shroff v. Tipco (Muir)*, accessed September 2014.
   http://www.canlii.org/en/on/onhrt/doc/2009/2009hrto1405/2009hrto1405.html

between management and employees or normal discussion between management and employees. It is not abnormal, nor should it be prohibited, activity for a supervisor to become socially involved with an employee. An invitation to dinner is not an invitation to a complaint. <u>The danger or the evil that is to be avoided is coerced or compelled social contact where the employee's refusal to participate may result in a loss of employment benefits.</u> Such coercion or compulsion may be overt or subtle but if any feature of employment becomes reasonably dependant on reciprocating a social relationship proffered by a member of management, then the overture becomes a condition of employment and may be considered to be discriminatory.

The decision of Professor Ratushny in *Aragona v. Elegant Lamp Company Ltd. and Fillipitto* (1982) 3 CHRR D/1109 at p. D/110 commented to the effect that it may be difficult to draw the line to demonstrate at what point a reference which is "crude or in bad taste" may be crossed:

Thus, sexual references which are crude or in bad taste are not necessarily sufficient to constitute a contravention of section 4 of the Code on the basis of sex. The line of sexual harassment is crossed only where the conduct may be reasonably construed to create, as a condition of employment, a work environment which demands an unwarranted intrusion upon the employee's sexual dignity as a man or woman. The line will seldom be easy to draw ...

The same decision referenced the 1982 decision of the Board of Inquiry in *Torres v. Royal Kitchenware and Guercio* (Cumming) in which the conclusion was made that telling "sex jokes" would not be considered an offence under the Code:

There are some employers (and employees) who simply are very crude and who speak in bad taste in discussing in the workplace their relationship with the opposite sex, or in telling sex "jokes." It is not the intent, or effect, of the Human Rights Code, or the function of a Board of Inquiry, to pass judgment upon such persons. It is only "sexual harassment" that is unlawful conduct.

However, times change and what may have been considered permissible in 1982 will be viewed in a different context in 2014 as these words are written. In *Law v. Noonan* (Sanderson)[14] a Tribunal decision in March 2013, the employer's conduct in the telling of sexual jokes and also of conduct simulating sexual groping was found to be a violation of the Code resulting in a compensatory award of $3,000. The joke was described as follows:

In my view, it is not necessary to determine whether the respondent first told the vulgar joke to the applicant or repeated it after hearing it from another employee. In any case, there is no dispute that the respondent told a highly offensive sexual joke to an employee. The respondent's evidence was that the joke was selected because it was offensive and that

---

14 *Law v. Noonan* (Sanderson), accessed September 2014.
  http://www.canlii.org/en/on/onhrt/doc/2013/2013hrto437/2013hrto437.html

the applicant stated it was disgusting. Consequently, I find the respondent knew or ought to have known that telling this joke to the applicant would be unwelcome.

Both the joke and the sexual gesture were each determined to be violations of the Code:

I find that the respondent on one occasion told a vulgar sexual joke and on another occasion made a sexual joke in connection with a sexual gesture (self-groping) that he knew or ought to have known were offensive.... I find that the jokes and gesture violated section 7(2) of the Code.

Many of the earlier cases must be read in the context of the era in which they were decided. In *Aragona v. Elegant Lamp* (Ratushny) 3 CHRR D/1109, a decision made in August of 1982, the Board offered an example of behaviour in which a positive comment was made of a female worker's legs. The decision noted that a woman who wore a miniskirt to work "might well invite such comments" and a clear statement would be expected from her to advise that such comments were unwelcome, following which, a repetition of such a similar statement "could well cross the line." It is difficult to believe that this could be an accurate statement of the law today. The passage reflecting this view is virtually comedic in today's context:

For example, a comment about one's legs might be returned with a gratitude for a perceived compliment, with repartee or with a clear statement that such comments are not acceptable to the individual involved. Subsequent comments in the face of the last response could well cross the line of harassment. Of course, much will depend on the circumstances. A businessman who wears shorts to work or a secretary who wears a miniskirt might well invite such comments.

The same case considered a work environment in which words that would normally be considered offensive were apparently accepted and "enjoyed" by other employees. The Board noted that such conduct was the norm of the workplace:

Where there is general acceptance but where an individual employee does not care to participate, that feeling should be expressly directly and unambiguously. The objective standard could then be applied to **that individual** *in light of the* **additional fact** *of expressed disapproval. (emphasis added in original text - ed.)*

The Tribunal in S*mith v. Menzies Chrysler* (Chadha)[15] spoke to the employer's obligation to ensure a proper working environment:

While the complainant may be culpable for his own use of inappropriate language, this does not excuse or nullify Graham's discriminatory misconduct towards the complainant. Nor does it excuse the failure of Lyons, Clark Menzies and the corporate respondent to take steps to address the existence of a poisoned work environment. The evidence established that

---

15 *Smith v. Menzies Chrysler* (Chadha), accessed September 2014.
   http://www.canlii.org/en/on/onhrt/doc/2009/2009hrto1936/2009hrto1936.html

the complainant was disgusted by, and protested, when Graham subjected him to crude remarks and exhibitionism. Based on this evidence, it is apparent that the respondents knew, or ought to have known, that Graham's behaviour was unwelcome. Further, regardless of whether anyone objects to, or everyone participates in, sexually charged behaviour, the employer has a duty to take steps to ensure the workplace is free from vexatious comments or conduct.

The Tribunal's decision continued to note the onus rests on the employer to ensure this standard is met:

> *Management at Menzies Chrysler had a responsibility to set a professional tone in the workplace and to ensure that staff is aware that discriminatory and harassing behaviour is unacceptable in the workplace. Instead, management at Menzies Chrysler not only tolerated sexual comments and conduct in the workplace, but also engaged in these behaviours. I find that management at Menzies Chrysler condoned the sexualized work environment. I further find that management failed to take the complainant's concerns seriously and/or to properly investigate the complainant's concerns. Human rights jurisprudence has established that an employer is under a duty to take reasonable steps to address allegations of discrimination or harassment in the workplace and that a failure to do so will itself result in liability under the Code ... As such, the corporate respondent breached its duty to provide the complainant with a workplace free of discrimination and harassment and failed to take adequate steps to address the poisoned work environment.*

The 2013 decision of the Court of Queen's Bench of Alberta in *Clarke v. Syncrude Canada Ltd.*[16] of Mr. Justice Macleod speaks to the changing view in society's acceptance of such conduct:

> *[35] The cases provided by Syncrude ... certainly provide evidence of a trend towards a decreasing tolerance for sexual harassment.*

The prevailing theme of a new order was repeated in the decision of the Divisional Court in its May 2013 decision of *Professional Institute of the Public Service of Canada v. Communications, Energy and Paperworkers' Union of Canada*[17] reviewing an arbitrator's award under the terms of a collective agreement reversed the arbitral award of suspension and reinstatement and found that termination of employment was the appropriate remedy.

The decision spoke strongly of the employer's need to provide a safe work environment, particularly with reference to the recent amendments to the *Occupational Health and Safety Act* and it is submitted, although in an arbitral context (i.e., a case which went to arbitration in the context of a unionized work place), is reflective of a more strict approach to conduct of sexual harassment in a modern work environment:

---

16 *Clarke v. Syncrude Canada Ltd.*, accessed September 2014.
   http://www.canlii.org/en/ab/abqb/doc/2013/2013abqb252/2013abqb252.html
17 *Professional Institute of the Public Service of Canada v. Communications, Energy and Paperworkers'
   Union of Canada*, accessed September 2014. http://www.canlii.org/en/on/onscdc/doc/2013/
   2013onsc2725/2013onsc2725.html

The arbitrator's reasons demonstrate that he was keenly aware of Mr. Haniff's lack of remorse and insight. Yet he chose to reinstate Mr. Haniff on the basis of what he regarded as two "significant" pieces of evidence. First, another cleaner was able to get Mr. Haniff to stop sexually harassing her when she threatened him with violence by showing him her fist and the same cleaner also testified that the Complainant was a strong woman who could stand up for herself. Second, the Complainant did not want Mr. Haniff discharged.

[26] Both these considerations were irrelevant and represent a dangerous step backwards in the law surrounding the treatment of sexual misconduct in the workplace. It is not the responsibility of employees to protect themselves from being sexually harassed or assaulted by being strong or threatening violence. Employees are entitled to a workplace that is free from sexual harassment and employers have a responsibility to ensure that their employees are not exposed to this type of behaviour. The legislature has reinforced these obligations in Bill 168, which involved a series of amendments to the Occupational Health and Safety Act that deal with violence and harassment in the workplace. In Re Zehrs Markets and U.F.C.W., Local 1977 (8494) (2010), 202 L.A.C. (4th) 308, at para. 33, another Ontario arbitrator noted an employer's obligations under this legislation as follows:

> *At the same time, however, his failure to acknowledge wrongdoing is a serious aggravating factor. Nor should I disregard the likely consequences for the morale of the complainant and her co-workers, and for the Company's ability to carry out its obligations with respect to workplace violence and harassment under the Occupational Health and Safety Act and sexual harassment under the Ontario Human Rights Code, R.S.O. 1990, c. H.19, were I to return the grievor to the workplace notwithstanding his failure to admit to what he did and that it was wrong.*

The line may not only be fine, but one which shifts to reflect contemporary morals and expectations.

1.3 Family status complaints

One case attracting considerable attention recently is that of *Johnstone v. Canada Border Service Agency*.[18] The complainant (employee) had requested a revision to the hours of work due to child-care needs. The employer's required working hours were based on a schedule of five days on, three days off, which included shift work that was irregular and unpredictable.

The employee requested that she be allowed to work three day shifts of 13 hours each as she had been able to arrange for child care in this manner. This was revised by her to three day shifts at 12 hours each.

---

18 *Johnstone v. Canada Border Service Agency*, accessed September 2014.
   http://www.canlii.org/en/ca/chrt/doc/2010/2010chrt20/2010chrt20.html

The employer offered a regular shift of three days a week at ten hours each day plus an extra four hours. This meant that the employee would be relegated to part-time status. The employer took no steps to determine the degree of hardship it would suffer by accommodating the request. Its defence was accordingly not based on a test of "undue hardship," only that it had no legal obligation to accommodate the request.

The Human Rights Tribunal found that child-care responsibilities of this nature fit into the definition of "family status":

> *This Tribunal finds that the freedom to choose to become a parent is so vital that it should not be constrained by the fear of discriminatory consequences. As a society, Canada should recognize this fundamental freedom and support that choice wherever possible. For the employer, this means assessing situations such as Ms. Johnstone's on an individual basis and working together with her to create a workable solution that balances her parental obligations with her work opportunities, short of undue hardship.*

There was some issue as to whether the employee was required to meet a higher standard test to show a human rights violation based on family status by showing a "serious interference with a substantial serious parental duty or obligation," based on a prior case in British Columbia. This was rejected.

The employer was shown to have treated a parent requesting accommodation due to child-care needs differently from those employees making the comparable requests based on medical or religious grounds.

> *This Tribunal finds that Ms. Johnstone has made out a prima facie case of discrimination contrary to Sections 7 and 10 of the Act, in that CBSA engaged in a discriminatory and arbitrary practice in the course of employment that adversely differentiated Ms. Johnstone on the prohibited ground of family status. CBSA engaged in a discriminatory practice by establishing and pursuing an unwritten policy communicated to and followed by management that affected Ms. Johnstone's employment opportunities including, but not limited to promotion, training, transfer, and benefits on the prohibited ground of family status.*

> *[243] The policy and practice that CBSA established and pursued is based in a view that family status within the meaning of the Act does not include family obligations of the nature of Ms. Johnstone's. CBSA forced Ms. Johnstone to self-reduce to part-time status thereby adversely affecting her with respect to employment.*

The employer's application for review failed. On this first review the Federal Court agreed with the test used by the human rights adjudicator, stating that the test was "the employment rule interferes with an employee's ability to fulfill her substantial parental obligations in any realistic way." The employer's appeal to the Federal Court of Appeal failed.

The Federal Court of Appeal did offer some guidelines for future fact situations to determine whether the employer was under a duty to accommodate child-care requirements of its employee. This Court noted that the child-care issues must have "immutable or constructively immutable personal characteristics," ones which cannot be neglected without attracting legal consequences. Picking up the kids at hockey practice would not qualify:

> That being said, the precise types of childcare activities that are contemplated by the prohibited ground of family status need to be carefully considered. Prohibited grounds of discrimination generally address immutable or constructively immutable personal characteristics, and the types of childcare needs which are contemplated under family status must therefore be those which have an immutable or constructively immutable characteristic.
>
> [69] It is also important not to trivialize human rights legislation by extending human rights protection to personal family choices, such as participation of children in dance classes, sports events like hockey tournaments, and similar voluntary activities. These types of activities would be covered by family status according to one of the counsel who appeared before us, and I disagree with such an interpretation.
>
> [70] The childcare obligations that are contemplated under family status should be those that have immutable or constructively immutable characteristics, such as those that form an integral component of the legal relationship between a parent and a child. As a result, the childcare obligations at issue are those which a parent cannot neglect without engaging his or her legal liability. Thus a parent cannot leave a young child without supervision at home in order to pursue his or her work, since this would constitute a form of neglect, which in extreme examples could even engage ss. 215(1) ... [71] Even conduct which meets the criminal standard, minimal as it is, does not necessarily meet other legal standards of childcare, such as those found in the child welfare legislation of the various provinces or in article 599 of the Quebec Civil Code. Put another way, the parental obligations whose fulfillment is protected by the Canadian Human Rights Act are those whose non-fulfillment engages the parent's legal responsibility to the child.
>
> [72] Voluntary family activities, such as family trips, participation in extracurricular sports events, etc. do not have this immutable characteristic since they result from parental choices rather than parental obligations. These activities would not normally trigger a claim to discrimination resulting in some obligation to accommodate by an employer ...
>
> [73] I note that there is no fundamental discrepancy between an interpretation of family status as including childcare obligations that engage the parent's legal responsibility for the child and Parliament's intent in including that prohibited ground of discrimination

in the Canadian Human Rights Act. Protection from discrimina-
tion for childcare obligations flows from family status in the same
manner that protection against discrimination on the basis of
pregnancy flows from the sex of the individual. In both cases, the
individual would not require accommodation were it not for the
underlying ground (family status or sex) on which they were ad-
versely affected.

[74] In conclusion, the ground of family status in the Canadian
Human Rights Act includes parental obligations which engage the
parent's legal responsibility for the child, such as childcare obli-
gations, as opposed to personal choices. Defining the scope of the
prohibited ground in terms of the parent's legal responsibility (i)
ensures that the protection offered by the legislation addresses im-
mutable (or constructively immutable) characteristics of the fam-
ily relationship captured under the concept of family status, (ii)
allows the right to be defined in terms of clearly understandable
legal concepts, and (iii) places the ground of family status in the
same category as other enumerated prohibited grounds of dis-
crimination such as sex, colour, disability, etc.

In a decision which was released contemporaneously, the Federal
Court in *Canadian National Railway Company v. Seeley*[19] stated that
child-care requirements fall within the protections of family status. In this
case, the employee, a mother of two children, was asked to move from
Jasper, Alberta, to Vancouver, BC, without any indication of the length of
time she would be in Vancouver:

The Tribunal found that Ms. Seeley had made out a case of prima
facie discrimination since she had demonstrated that she was the
parent of two children, she could not rely on her husband for the
childcare needs of these children as a result of his own work sched-
ule for CN, that she was told to temporarily move to Vancouver
"with no information with regard to how long she would have to
stay there or about housing arrangements once she arrived there,"
and that this temporary move "would disrupt her children's care
and that it would be impossible for her to make arrangements for
appropriate child care": Tribunal's decision at para. 123.

[20] The Tribunal further found that CN had not demonstrated
that the accommodation sought by Ms. Seeley would cause it
undue hardship under the third element of the three-step test set
out in British Columbia (Public Service Employee Relations Com-
mission) v. BCGSEU, 1999 CanLII 652 (SCC), [1999] 3 S.C.R. 3
("Meiorin") at paras. 54 and 55. The Tribunal concluded from the
evidence "that CN was not sensitive to the Complainant's situa-
tion" and "did not answer her many requests for some form of ac-
commodation and did not even meet or contact her to discuss her
situation ... ": Tribunal's decision at para. 150.

---

19 *Canadian National Railway Company v. Seeley*, accessed September 2014.
   http://www.canlii.org/en/ca/fca/doc/2014/2014fca111/2014fca111.html

The court added the following words to define "family status":

> *If one looks to the ordinary meaning of the words, the definition of the word "family" in the Canadian Oxford Dictionary [2nd edition] includes "the members of a household esp. parents and their children." The definition of the word "status" includes "a person's legal standing which determines his or her rights and duties." The two words taken together amount to more than a mere descriptor of a parent of a child and also reference the obligations of a parent to care for the child.*

> *[68] Finally, it is difficult to have regard to family without giving thought to children in the family and the relationship between parents and children. The singular most important aspect of that relationship is the parents' care for children. It seems to me that if Parliament intended to exclude parental childcare obligations, it would have chosen language that clearly said so.*

The Ontario Human Rights Tribunal in *Devaney v. ZRV Holdings Limited*[20] agreed that the protections of the Code and the definition of family status extended to the need for the complainant to care for his elderly parent who was in need of medical treatment. The applicant must show that the obligation is one which is required, as opposed to voluntary:

> *Each case must be determined based on its own facts and circumstances. Applying the above principles to the facts of the case at hand, I find that, in order to make out a prima facie case of discrimination on the basis of family status, the applicant must establish that the respondents' attendance requirements had an adverse impact on the applicant because of absences that were* **required** *as a result of the applicant's responsibilities as his mother's primary caregiver. I say "required" because I agree with the respondents that if it is the caregiver's choice, rather than family responsibilities, that preclude the caregiver from meeting his or her employer's attendance requirements, a prima facie case of discrimination on the basis of family status is not established.*

In this case the employer failed to show that it offered procedural and substantive accommodation and the employee's case succeeded. An award of $15,000 of compensation was made.

In *Hicks v. Human Resources and Skills Development Canada*,[21] the complainant was moved by his employer from Nova Scotia to Ottawa. His wife did not move due to the need to care for her ailing mother. The employer maintained a policy for reimbursement of dual residence expenses which it denied in this circumstance as the complainant's mother-in-law did not meet the definition of eligibility. A successful claim was made based on adverse treatment due to family status.

---

20 *Devaney v. ZRV Holdings Limited*, accessed September 2014.
  http://www.canlii.org/en/on/onhrt/doc/2012/2012hrto1590/2012hrto1590.html
21 *Hicks v. Human Resources and Skills Development Canada*, accessed September 2014.
  http://www.canlii.org/en/ca/chrt/doc/2013/2013chrt20/2013chrt20.html

The tribunal noted the interpretation of "family status" to include "duties and obligations that may arise within the family":

> However, jurisprudence has recognized that the ground protects the absolute status of being or not being in a family relationship; the relative status of who one's family members are; the particular circumstances or characteristics of one's family; and, the duties and obligations that may arise within the family.

As noted by the Federal Court of Appeal, not all duties that arise within the family context will engage a protected right. The duty must be one which is just that, a legal duty for which legal consequences will flow if the employee cannot meet his or her obligation.

The Supreme Court of Canada in *B. v. Ontario (Human Rights Commission)* considered an unusual fact situation in interpreting the words "family status" and "marital status" of the Ontario Code. The complainant, Mr. A, was the brother-in-law of the two owners of his employer, Mr. B and Mr. C, who were uncles to the daughter of Mr. and Mrs. A. Mr. B was confronted by his niece and his sister, Ms. A and Mrs. A, that he had sexually molested Ms. A. He, in turn, terminated the employment of Mr. A, a long-term employee approaching retirement.

The issue was whether the Code's protections applied to the specific identity of the complainant as a family member or whether the words were limited to distinctions based on the fact that the complainant has a certain type of family or marital status.

The Supreme Court found that this was the case and, hence, in favour of the applicant, Mr. A:

> There is little doubt that discrimination on the basis of <u>absolute status</u> (e.g., married/single) is prohibited by the Code. Indeed, this is discrimination in its classic form. Discrimination on the basis of <u>relative status</u> will also be caught by the Code where there is some rule of general application that results in differential treatment of a particular sub-group. Aptly named by the respondents as "group identity" complaints, the most common example is a general anti-nepotism policy in the employment context. Discrimination in this context occurs where the complainant's situation corresponds to that of a sub-class of persons who share an absolute status (e.g., married employees who adopt their husbands' surnames). To this point, the case law is not in conflict. All would agree that policies employer actions of general application that provide differential treatment to a sub-category of married persons would fall within the scope of "marital status." The Brossard line of cases parts ways with those that follow Cashin in the second type of relative status discrimination, the so-called "particular identity" complaints. These complaints involve the differential treatment of an individual based on a characteristic of the person's spouse that is objectionable to the employer.

Many jurisdictions which offer protection to "family status" in employment do not offer a definition of the term. This is the case for BC, Alberta, Manitoba, Ontario, Yukon, and Northwest Territories.

- *Saskatchewan's Code offers this definition:*

  (h.1) "family status" means the status of being in a parent and child relationship and, for the purposes of this clause:

  (i) "child" means son, daughter, stepson, stepdaughter, adopted child and person to whom another person stands in place of a parent;

  (ii) "parent" means father, mother, stepfather, stepmother, adoptive parent and person who stands in place of a parent to another person.

- *Nova Scotia and Prince Edward Island define the term to mean "the status of being in a parent and child relationship."*

- *Nunavut uses the words "the status of being related to another person by blood, marriage, or adoption."*

- *Newfoundland's statute defines the relationship as "the status of being in a parent and child relationship and, for the purpose of this paragraph, 'child' includes an adopted child and 'parent' includes an adoptive parent."*

While these statutes may define the ambit of the family members, the case law sets out the duties and obligations which are protected.

New Brunswick remains the sole jurisdiction not to offer protection on this ground.

2. Subtle Forms of Discrimination Complaints

Other cases of discrimination may not be so evident on the surface. In any case, alleging discriminatory conduct, it is clear that the employee may offer evidence which is systemic in nature to prove the case, even where the complainant is an individual. As Justice Abella stated in the Supreme Court of Canada decision in *Moore v. British Columbia (Education).*[22]

> *Having first found that Jeffrey had suffered discrimination at the hands of the District, the Tribunal then considered whether the broader policies of the District and the Province constituted systemic discrimination. I think this flows from the fact that it approached discrimination in a binary way: individual and systemic. It was, however, neither necessary nor conceptually helpful to divide discrimination into these two discrete categories. A practice is discriminatory whether it has an unjustifiably adverse*

---

22 *Moore v. British Columbia* (Education), accessed September 2014.
  http://www.canlii.org/en/ca/scc/doc/2012/2012scc61/2012scc61.html

impact on a single individual or systemically on several: Griggs v. Duke Power Co., 401 U.S. 424 (1971). The only difference is quantitative, that is, the number of people disadvantaged by the practice.

[59] In Canadian National Railway Co. v. Canada (Canadian Human Rights Commission), 1987 CanLII 109 (SCC), [1987] 1 S.C.R. 1114, this Court first identified "systemic discrimination" by name. It defined it as "practices or attitudes that have, whether by design or impact, the effect of limiting an individual's or a group's right to the opportunities generally available because of attributed rather than actual characteristics" (p. 1138). Notably, however, the designation did not change the analysis. The considerations and evidence at play in a group complaint may undoubtedly differ from those in an individual complaint, but the focus is always on whether the complainant has suffered arbitrary adverse effects based on a prohibited ground.

[60] The inquiry is into whether there is discrimination, period. The question in every case is the same: does the practice result in the claimant suffering arbitrary — or unjustified — barriers on the basis of his or her membership in a protected group. Where it does, discrimination will be established.

As was noted by the BC Human Rights Tribunal in *Cole and Joseph obo others v. Northern Health Authority and others*:[23]

Systemic discrimination was described in Canadian National Railway Co. v. Canada (Canadian Human Rights Commission), 1987 CanLII 109 (SCC), [1987] 1 S.C.R. 1114, where the Court held:

In other words, systemic in an employment context is discrimination that results from the simple operation of established procedures of recruitment, hiring and promotion, none of which is necessarily designed to promote discrimination. The discrimination is then reinforced by the very exclusion of the disadvantaged group because the exclusion fosters the belief, both within and outside the group, that the exclusion is the result of "natural" forces ... To combat systemic discrimination, it is essential to create a climate in which both negative practices and negative attitudes can be challenged and discouraged.

It is clear that evidence of systemic discrimination can be used to support an individual claim. The Canadian Human Rights Tribunal in *Desmarais v. Correctional Service of Canada*[24] came to the same conclusion:

[101] It is worth noting that the Court in Moore overturned the Tribunal's decision to award a number of systemic remedies, however it did not preclude the Tribunal from considering systemic evidence in its decision to substantiate the complaint. In fact the Court explicitly recognized the Tribunal's ability to consider systemic evidence

---

23 *Cole and Joseph obo others v. Northern Health Authority and others*, accessed September 2014.
   http://www.canlii.org/en/bc/bchrt/doc/2014/2014bchrt26/2014bchrt26.html
24 *Desmarais v. Correctional Service of Canada*, accessed September 2014.
   http://www.canlii.org/en/ca/chrt/doc/2014/2014chrt5/2014chrt5.html

in order to determine whether Jeffrey had suffered discrimination: Moore at para. 63.

[102] The Respondent seeks to strike the allegations of systemic discrimination outside of the Complainant's periods of incarceration with CSC on a preliminary basis, a discretion which, as stated above, the Tribunal must exercise only in the "clearest of cases." Were the Tribunal to grant the motion as requested, this would prevent the Complainant from relying on any evidence of systemic discrimination at CSC outside of the periods of his incarceration to support his own claim of discrimination. The Court in Moore explicitly recognizes that systemic evidence "can be instrumental in establishing a human rights complaint": Moore at para. 65. There is no question that evidence of systemic discrimination against intellectually disabled inmates by the Respondent both during and outside of Mr. Desmarais' periods of incarceration may support the Complainant's individual complaint of discrimination.

The *Canadian Human Rights Act* bars a claim which is:

40.1 (b) … based solely on statistical information that purports to show that members of one or more designated groups are underrepresented in the employer's workforce.

3. Limitation Periods

The time to commence a claim varies from jurisdiction to jurisdiction. Some allow for an extension of the stated time period, usually conditioned by a requirement that the delay was incurred in good faith and that the employer will suffer no prejudice:

- *BC has the shortest limitation period of six months. It allows for an extension wherein the public interest and no prejudice is shown.*

- *Nunavut's period is set at two years and also allows an extension where the delay was occasioned in good faith and no prejudice has been suffered.*

- *Manitoba sets a one-year proscription period and allows for an extension where there is no prejudice and it is an individual who seeks the extra time and not the Commission.*

- *New Brunswick and Saskatchewan allow for a one-year period and a general discretion to extend without any set guidelines on the face of the statute.*

- *Prince Edward Island, Alberta, and Newfoundland fix a one-year absolute period.*

- *Quebec's Charter requires the case be commenced within two years and there is no provision for an extension.*

- *Nova Scotia and Ontario set a one-year period and each allow for extensions where there is no prejudice. Ontario requires the applicant to also show good faith. Ontario allows for a human rights claim within a companion civil action in which case the limitation period is two years.*

- *Northwest Territories has a two-year period with extensions available on the same terms as Ontario, which is the same law as the Yukon, apart from the set time period which is 18 months.*

- *The federal law sets the filing period as one year and allows for a residual discretion to extend to the commission.*

5

The Difference between Human Rights Claims and Employment Law Wrongful Dismissal Cases

There are many major differences between human rights claims and wrongful dismissal cases. Unlike common-law claims, which originate from "implied" rights in the workplace, all human rights cases must find the origin of the case in the relevant human rights statute. Each jurisdiction in Canada has a statute setting out the definition of what human rights are protected and how the case may be pursued.

In all jurisdictions but Ontario, the case must be started by the individual filing a complaint setting out the essential reasons for the case and the remedy that is sought. There are also limitation periods, as set out in Chapter 4, for starting the case, which are important because not filing the case in time may result in the case being lost without a hearing. The case is brought before an "administrative tribunal" which typically consists of one person who holds a hearing similar to a civil trial.

Ontario law allows a choice to the applicant to use only the human rights process or alternatively, to advance a claim for a human rights violation in a civil court where such a claim is made with a companion action, usually a wrongful dismissal case, although it can be any other civil claim. Ontario is the only jurisdiction to allow this.

All human rights cases in other jurisdictions must use the administrative process defined in the relevant human rights code.

1. Proving the Case

It is important that you understand the process of proving a human rights complaint.

The employee's claim proceeds first. Evidence will be called by the complainant and any relevant witnesses. The employee's case must succeed in proving only a *prima facie* case, which in real words, means one which shows a case that is enough to justify success in the case, if believed as being credible. Presuming that this evidence is proven, the employer must call its case to rebut the employee's case and explain its actions.

For example, if the employee argued that she was not hired because of her gender and showed that she was well qualified for the position and that of the ten people hired in the last two years, all were men, the employer may call evidence to show why it did not consider her as a viable candidate due to her past experience or bad references. The employer will have the chance to prove that the reason for not hiring the person was a genuine business one and not motivated or influenced by gender.

At the end of the day, it is the employee who has the obligation to prove the case.

Most statutes do not define the burden of proof, although Manitoba, Saskatchewan, and Prince Edward Island do. Even where defined, it is true that the complainant has the burden of proof to show adverse treatment and the employer must prove its defence, as the case may be.

Saskatchewan's statute specifically defines the onus of proof as reversed to the employer, once a code violation has been proven.

2. The Absence of Direct Evidence

Human rights cases have recognized the difficulty in proving a human rights violation and have developed their own jurisprudence or case law to deal with this issue.

It has been recognized in precedent cases that there is very rarely direct evidence of a human rights violation. Employers do not overtly state to an employee that "we have decided to terminate your employment because of your religion" or race or gender as the case may be. For this reason, in human rights cases, the tribunal will make its conclusions of evidence based on "reasonable inference."

The following example is not an employment case, but the principle of how the evidence is analyzed still applies with equal force. In *Shaw v.*

Phibb[1] (confirmed on appeal) the following was stated by the Divisional Court (an appeal court in Ontario):

> *Many discrimination cases, such as this case, do not involve direct evidence that a complainant's colour or race was a factor in the incident in question. A tribunal must draw reasonable inferences from proven facts.*

The evidentiary process was summarized by the Divisional Court, in approving of the analysis of the Human Rights Tribunal as follows in a case in which the evidence is not direct:

> *In cases where discrimination must be proved by circumstantial evidence, there are no bright lines. The Tribunal must determine what reasonable inferences can be drawn from proven facts. These are difficult, nuanced cases that are important to both the parties, to society and the neighbourhoods in which we live. The Tribunal notes (at para. 17):*
>
> *In this case, as in many cases alleging racial discrimination, there is no direct evidence that race was a factor in the officer's decision to take the actions that he did. As a result, the issue of whether the officer's actions amount to racial discrimination in violation of the Code falls to be determined in accordance with the following well-established principles applicable to circumstantial evidence cases.*

You may see that this is very different from how a judge proceeds in a civil case and how it reflects the difficulty inherent in proving a human rights violation and to this extent, eases the process in favour of the complainant.

To prove a human rights wrong has been committed, the employee does not need to show that the offensive conduct was the sole and only cause of the wrongdoing. You, as the complainant, must prove only that the decision was influenced by a human rights violation. For example, if the employer stated that the termination was due to significant performance issues and that normally it would retrain and teach the employee how to improve, but did not do so due to the age of the employee, a successful case will be made. The decision was thus influenced by a human rights wrongdoing.

As the employee, you don't need to show that the actions in question were intended to be malicious or intentional. As long as the human rights statute was violated, it doesn't matter that the employer was not aware that it was offside the law.

3. Motion to Dismiss before Full Hearing

If you are self-represented in either BC or Ontario, you should prepare for motion to dismiss type of pre-hearing motion. This form of motion is more

---

1 *Shaw v. Phibb*, accessed September 2014.
   http://www.canlii.org/en/on/onca/doc/2012/2012onca155/2012onca155.html

common in BC and Ontario which are direct user access systems. There is no screening system in place such as is the case in other jurisdictions in which the human rights commission has carriage of the case. Many users in these two jurisdictions are self-represented and often have commenced cases without proper legal advice and the claims reflect this.

Similar to BC and Ontario, Nunavut has a direct user access system. Similar to the motion to dismiss process, Nunavut gives its tribunal the power to dismiss a claim where it is shown to be without merit and also where a reasonable offer has been submitted.

The statute in BC states as follows:

> *Section 27(1)(b) and (c) provides:*
>
> (1) *A member or panel may, at any time after a complaint is filed and with or without a hearing, dismiss all or part of the complaint if that member or panel determines that any of the following apply: ...*
>
> (b) *the acts or omissions alleged in the complaint or that part of the complaint do not contravene the Code;*
>
> (c) *there is no reasonable prospect that the complaint will succeed.*

The process in BC under 27(1)b does not involve an assessment of the employer's case. The issue is simply one of determining if the applicant's allegations, on the face of the complaint, if proven, will show a contravention of the Code. The threshold for the employee's success in maintaining his or her case on this motion is low.

In the recent decision of *MacDonald v. Stevenson Luchies & Legh and another*,[2] the Human Rights Tribunal of BC stated the test as follows for a "no reasonable prospect of success" motion under the second provision of 27(1)c:

> *Under section 27(1)(c) of the Code, the Tribunal conducts a preliminary assessment of whether there is no reasonable prospect that the complaint will succeed ... This provision creates a gate-keeping function that permits the Tribunal, on the basis of a preliminary assessment, to determine if the matter warrants the time and expense of a hearing. This is a discretionary exercise by the Tribunal and does not require factual findings; merely an assessment of the evidence submitted by the parties ... leave to appeal ref'd, [2010] SCCA No. 217, paras. 25, 31. The threshold for such a review is low. The Complainant must only show that his complaint is not speculation or conjecture: Hill para. 27. As set out in more detail in Rajigadu v. UBC and others, 2012 BCHRT 7 (CanLII), 2012 BCHRT 7, paras. 74-78, this involves an assessment, on the whole of the material before the Tribunal, whether it takes the complaint "out of the realm*

---

2   *MacDonald v. Stevenson Luchies & Legh and another*, accessed September 2014. http://www.canlii.org/en/bc/bchrt/doc/2014/2014bchrt69/2014bchrt69.html

of conjecture," or whether there is "no reasonable prospect that findings of fact that would support the complaint could be made on a balance of probabilities after a full hearing of the evidence."

In this instance, where there were competing versions of the evidence put forward on the motion, the Tribunal thought it best to allow the evidence be tested by a full hearing, although as the decision stated, this is not an automatic conclusion where the evidence from each party differs:

> *Differences in the parties' versions of events is not necessarily enough to require that a complaint must proceed to hearing for resolution ... Even where there are differences in the parties' respective versions of events, this does not necessarily mean that the time and expense of a full evidentiary hearing is required or warranted ... Nor is the fact that a complaint may raise issues of credibility ... However, in my opinion, the complaint will turn on factual findings which are best left to be determined in the context of a hearing where evidence is received under oath, tested by cross-examination, and subjected to full legal argument and submissions.*

The leading case on this issue of "no reasonable chance of success" is the British Columbia Court of Appeal decision in *Workers' Compensation Appeal Tribunal v. Hill.*[3]

> *It is useful to describe the nature of an application under s. 27 of the Code to provide context for the appellants' arguments. That provision creates a gate-keeping function that permits the Tribunal to conduct preliminary assessments of human rights complaints with a view to removing those that do not warrant the time and expense of a hearing. It is a discretionary exercise that does not require factual findings. Instead, a Tribunal member assesses the evidence presented by the parties with a view to determining if there is no reasonable prospect the complaint will succeed. The threshold is low. The complainant must only show the evidence takes the case out of the realm of conjecture. If the application is dismissed, the complaint proceeds to a full hearing before the Tribunal. If it is granted, the complaint comes to an end, subject to the complainant's right to seek judicial review.*

When presented with a motion to dismiss under this subsection, the employee should submit his or her best evidence to be assured of maintaining the complaint. It is the employer that must show to the tribunal that the employee's case has no reasonable chance of success on this motion. As was stated in *Bowen v. British Columbia Lottery Corporation (BCLC):*[4]

> *However, under s. 27 of the Code, the Tribunal does not determine whether the complainant has established a prima facie case of*

3 *Workers' Compensation Appeal Tribunal v. Hill*, accessed September 2014.
   http://www.canlii.org/en/bc/bcca/doc/2011/2011bcca49/2011bcca49.html
4 *Bowen v. British Columbia Lottery Corporation*, accessed September 2014.
   http://www.canlii.org/en/bc/bchrt/doc/2014/2014bchrt109/2014bchrt109.html

discrimination: The burden is not on Ms. Bowen to establish a prima facie case. Rather, the burden is on BCLC to show that she has no reasonable prospect of success in doing so.

Although the onus is on the moving employer, the employee should nonetheless understand the need for *prima facie* case and prepare his or her evidence accordingly. As was stated in *Yu v. Kerrisdale Equipment and others:*[5]

> *For his complaint to succeed at a hearing, Mr. Yu would have to establish a prima facie case of discrimination ... To establish prima facie discrimination, a complainant must show that he has a characteristic protected from discrimination; that he has experienced adverse treatment; and that the protected characteristic was, or it is reasonable to infer that it was, a factor in the adverse treatment. Once a prima facie case has been established, the burden shifts to the respondent to justify the conduct or practice. If it cannot be justified, discrimination will be found to have occurred ... On an application to dismiss, the burden is not on Mr. Yu to establish a prima facie case of discrimination, but rather it is on the Respondent to show that he has no reasonable prospect of success in doing so.*

The Code also allows for a motion to dismiss under section 27(1)d(ii). The basis of this submission is that proceeding with the case would not further the purposes of the Code. This involves broader public policy issues. One argument in favour of dismissal is that the employer has taken reasonable steps to investigate and resolve the dispute. A second is where the complainant has engaged in misconduct.

Ontario's rules allow for a summary hearing to determine if the case should be dismissed before a full hearing. Like the sub-rule in BC, the test is "no reasonable chance of success":

> *19A.1 The Tribunal may hold a summary hearing, on its own initiative or at the request of a party, on the question of whether an Application should be dismissed in whole or in part on the basis that there is no reasonable prospect that the Application or part of the Application will succeed.*

In *Dabic v. Windsor Police Service,*[6] noted that there are, in essence two types of arguments that can be made by the employer to dismiss the claim without a hearing:

- *Just as in the case in BC under the first rule, one submission that the employer can make is to presume the allegations in the claim are true and proceed then to argue that no violation of the Code is made out in law.*

- *The second type of argument is that the evidence cannot meet the test required for a valid human rights complaint. This could involve*

---

5 *Yu v. Kerrisdale Equipment and others*, accessed September 2014.
   http://www.canlii.org/en/bc/bchrt/doc/2014/2014bchrt63/2014bchrt63.html
6 *Dabic v. Windsor Police Service*, accessed September 2014.
   http://www.canlii.org/en/on/onhrt/doc/2010/2010hrto1994/2010hrto1994.html

a submission that the employee can offer no evidence to connect the alleged wrongdoing to the employer or that the employee has otherwise not made out a factual basis of the complaint.

An example of a successful motion to dismiss is that of *MacMaster v. Ubisoft Toronto*.[7] In this case, the employee asserted that she was adversely treated due to her financial status, which is not a ground of a human rights violation. This showed that there was clearly no chance of success.

The test for a summary hearing was refined in *Forde v. Elementary Teachers' Federation of Ontario*:[8]

> *The applicant has referred to the concept of prima facie discrimination. In my view, this concept is not helpful in interpreting the Tribunal's summary hearing rule. In human rights law, prima facie discrimination has been used to mean various things. In some contexts … the term is used to refer to what claimant must show to avoid having a claim dismissed without requiring a respondent to call evidence. In others … it refers to whether, assuming the allegations to be true, there is discrimination. In yet others … it refers to what is required for a claimant to demonstrate discrimination within the meaning of the Code. In my view, it is much more helpful and understandable to parties to simply speak in the summary hearing context about whether there is a reasonable prospect the application will succeed as set out in Dabic. Accordingly, whether there is a reasonable prospect the applicant can prove a violation of the Code is the issue that was explained in the Case Assessment Direction and on the telephone during the summary hearing.*

---

7 *MacMaster v. Ubisoft Toronto*, accessed September 2014.
   http://www.canlii.org/en/on/onhrt/doc/2011/2011hrto627/2011hrto627.html
8 *Forde v. Elementary Teachers' Federation of Ontario*, accessed September 2014.
   http://www.canlii.org/en/on/onhrt/doc/2011/2011hrto1389/2011hrto1389.html

6
General Damage Awards in Each Province and Territory

This chapter will help you understand the various damage award cases with specific examples for each province and territory.

1. Compensation for Injured Feelings

Each statute will apply its own wording for the compensation for injured feelings type of award. Ontario uses the vocabulary of "injury to dignity, feelings, and self-respect." The essential purpose of each jurisdiction is the same, namely, to allow for an award to compensate the victim for injured feelings.

All jurisdictions have stated that this damage sum to be awarded is not intended to be punitive, that is, intended to punish the offender, but rather is intended to compensate the victim for the offensive actions.

The range of the award will reflect the conduct in question and the impact on the applicant, which is viewed objectively. The high side of damage awards for injured feelings have been in the vicinity of $25,000 to $45,000 in Ontario.

Ontario's Code was amended in June of 2008. You should be aware that the prior version of the Code contained a provision which allowed for a damage award up to $10,000 for "mental anguish" due to willful or reckless conduct. There was some initial debate as to whether this limited the claim for emotional suffering to a cap of $10,000. Ultimately it was determined that this was not the law. This former provision was read to mean that a further sum up to $10,000 could be ordered where the conduct was willful or reckless, in addition to the usual damage claim for injured feelings.

When reviewing older cases dealing with the former Code, it is important to keep this in mind as some of the early cases stated that the maximum sum for emotional distress was set at $10,000, an incorrect conclusion. This provision allowing for damages for "mental anguish" was eliminated from the modern Code as of June 2008. There may be reported cases after this date, which deal with the old law.

1.1 Damages presumed

A damage award may be made because the Code has been breached, even without medical or other evidence to demonstrate the emotional harm that the victim has suffered. In this sense, damages to a person's integrity are "presumed."

The Board of Inquiry in an early decision of 1984 spoke to the damage assessment as being so presumed. Peter A. Cumming, now Mr. Justice Cumming of the Ontario Superior Court, in *Cameron v. Nel-Gor Castle Nursing Home and Nelson* (1984), 5 C.H.R.R. D/2170 stated as follows, referencing his prior decision of *Rosanna Torres v. Royalty Kitchenware Limited* (1982):

> There is a presumption in favour of the making of an award of special and general damages in human rights cases.
>
> Therefore, I think that a presumption in favour of awarding both special and general damages should be made by Boards of Inquiry. Compensatory awards should not be completely discretionary ... Since Parliament has indicated the desirability of compensating financial losses resulting from discriminatory practices, it seems only reasonable, in view of the philosophy underlying the legislation, that this should be the norm, applicable except if some good reason for not awarding compensation can be proved.

1.2 Damages for the loss of the right to be free of discrimination

In the same decision, Professor Cumming spoke to the damage sum to be awarded as damages. Following his assessment of the damages for injury to dignity or self-respect and the consequential need to reflect the seriousness of the injury, he spoke to the requirement that the damage sum also consider the loss of the human right in question:

An inherent, but separate, component of the general damage award should reflect the loss of the human right of equality of opportunity in employment. This is based upon the recognition that, independent of the actual monetary or personal losses suffered by the complainant whose human rights are infringed, the very human right which has been contravened has intrinsic value. The loss of this right is itself an independent injury which a complainant suffers.

Ontario's Divisional Court in *Scott v. Foster Wheeler* 8 CHRR D/4179 spoke to this issue in its review of the Board of Inquiry decision and came to the same decision that the breach of the Code, in this instance, a denial of an employment opportunity, should attract a damage claim:

When a person is denied recruitment because of his race that infringement of right should attract damages for insult to his dignity as well as the foregoing loss of income. Such damages flow directly from the denial or the discriminatory act.

Constance Backhouse, sitting as the Board of Inquiry in *Naraine*, set out her views of the damage award for a breach of the Code. At that time the Code contained an additional provision for damages for mental anguish where the conduct was reckless which is not relevant to this subject. The Board spoke to the issue of the damage award including compensation for the "loss of the right to be free from discrimination and the experience of victimization":

[39] In Ontario, human rights adjudicators have divided awards for general damages into two headings. The first branch covers non-pecuniary intangible damages arising from infringement of the Code. ... Boards have continued to award compensation under this branch for, among other things, loss of the right to be free from discrimination and the experience of victimization; ...

[40] The second branch covers compensation for complainants who have experienced mental anguish where the respondent has acted in a wilful or reckless manner. ... A clearer and more accurate characterization of this branch of recovery is that it represents "aggravated" damages. ...(this second branch is no longer in effect — ed.)

The decision in *Naraine* was upheld by the Divisional Court.[1] Leave to appeal or permission to appeal to the Court of Appeal[2] was granted on an unrelated ground and the remedy decision was amended on an unrelated ground. All this means that the referenced quoted words from *Naraine* remain good law and good authority to use in a hearing even today.

The Divisional Court in February of 2001, released its decision in *Shelter Corporation v. Ontario Human Rights Commission*[3] (leave to appeal to the Court of Appeal denied) spoke to the damage assessment for a human

---

1 *Ontario (Human Rights Commission) v. Ford Motor Co. of Canada Ltd.*, accessed September 2014. http://www.canlii.org/en/on/onscdc/doc/1999/1999canlii18727/1999canlii18727.html
2 *Ontario (Human Rights Commission) v. Naraine*, 2001, accessed September 2014. http://www.canlii.org/en/on/onca/doc/2001/2001canlii21234/2001canlii21234.html
3 *Shelter Corporation v. Ontario Human Rights Commission*, accessed September 2014. http://www.canlii.org/en/on/onsc/doc/2001/2001canlii28414/2001canlii28414.html

rights violation, then under 41(1)b of the former Code, as being designed to compensate for the "intrinsic value of the infringement" and for "the loss of the right to be free from discrimination and the experience of victimization."

The Divisional Court in *Adga Group Consultants Inc. v. Lane*[4] is a case involving adverse treatment due to a bipolar condition. It described the damage claim as being one to compensate for "the intrinsic value of the infringement or rights under the Code." Ferrier J., writing for the unanimous panel, stated:

> *Accordingly, the Tribunal does have the power under s.41(1)(b) to award what may be termed general damages to compensate for the intrinsic value of the infringement of rights under the Code; it is compensation for the loss of the right to be free from discrimination and the experience of victimization. (The operative section has since been revised. This revision has no impact on this principle — ed.)*

The Court identified the factors to be analyzed to set the general damage award were "humiliation; hurt feelings; the loss of self-respect; dignity and confidence by the complainant; the experience of victimization; and the seriousness of the offensive treatment."

In *Wilson v. Solis Mexican Foods Inc.*,[5] Grace J. of the Ontario Superior Court in a civil action in which human rights damages were claimed due to a Code violation of a physical disability, specifically a back ailment, reflected on the damage award where there was no medical evidence to support the claim and the sole evidence to support such a claim was the plaintiff's deposed evidence that she was "shocked, dismayed, and angered" by the conduct and also in the words of the trial judge, "she referred vaguely to 'the loss of dignity and loss of feelings of self-worth."

The court stated that the loss was not limited to the items referenced above and that the wording of the Code allowed for "compensation for the loss of the right to be free from discrimination and the experience of victimization" quoting from the Divisional Court decision in *Adga Group Consultants Inc. v. Lane*:

> *First in this case, the plaintiff lost "the right to be free from discrimination" and experienced "victimization." Second, the defendant's breach of the statute is serious. The defendant orchestrated the dismissal and was disingenuous at various times both before and during termination.*

An award of $20,000 was made.

The take-away from the above cases is that you can still recover a damage claim for loss of dignity and injured feelings without medical evidence. However, having medical evidence may be better as was the case in *G.G. v. Ontario Limited*[6] the Tribunal also considered the submissions made by the

---

4   *Adga Group Consultants Inc. v. Lane*, 2008, accessed September 2014.
     http://www.canlii.org/en/on/onscdc/doc/2008/2008canlii39605/2008canlii39605.html
5   *Wilson v. Solis Mexican Foods Inc.*, accessed September 2014.
     http://www.canlii.org/en/on/onsc/doc/2013/2013onsc5799/2013onsc5799.html
6   *G.G. v. Ontario Limited*, accessed September 2014.
     http://www.canlii.org/en/on/onhrt/doc/2012/2012hrto1197/2012hrto1197.html

respondents, namely that the actions were not premeditated, but rather were impulsive, that there was no medical evidence adduced by the complainant, the event was a singular occasion and stated that these factors would lessen the damages awarded. Just the same, $18,000 was awarded:

> I find the violation of the applicant's Code rights to be serious. It involved inappropriate physical touching and this physical touching continued notwithstanding that the applicant made it clear to the personal respondent that this conduct was unwanted. I find the applicant was particularly vulnerable given that the personal respondent was not only her supervisor but the owner of the company for which she worked. I find that the applicant was effectively forced to leave her employment by the behaviour of her employer. I accept the applicant's testimony that this discrimination affected and continues to affect the applicant's sense of dignity, feelings and self-respect.

> [26] I find that the fact that this was a single incident and one that was not premeditated lessens its relative seriousness. I find that the lack of medical evidence as to how the applicant has been affected and the fact that the applicant has not required medication or counseling lessens the weight I can give to her relatively brief evidence as to how the discrimination has affected her.

An award was made of $18,000 for injury to feelings, dignity, and self-respect in addition to an award of $11,940 for lost wages. This effectively covered the applicant's period of unemployment from June 11, 2009, to November 27, 2009.

The principles to be applied in setting the damage award for injured feelings and loss of dignity and self-respect were set out in *Arunachalam v. Best Buy*:[7]

> The Tribunal's jurisprudence over the two years since the new damages provision took effect has primarily applied two criteria in making the global evaluation of the appropriate damages for injury to dignity, feelings and self-respect: the objective seriousness of the conduct and the effect on the particular applicant who experienced discrimination …

> The first criterion recognizes that injury to dignity, feelings, and self-respect is generally more serious depending, objectively, upon what occurred. For example, dismissal from employment for discriminatory reasons usually affects dignity more than a comment made on one occasion. Losing long-term employment because of discrimination is typically more harmful than losing a new job. The more prolonged, hurtful, and serious harassing comments are, the greater the injury to dignity, feelings and self-respect.

> The second criterion recognizes the applicant's particular experience in response to the discrimination. Damages will be generally

---

7   *Arunachalam v. Best Buy*, 2010, accessed September 2014.
http://www.canlii.org/en/on/onhrt/doc/2010/2010hrto1880/2010hrto1880.html

*at the high end of the relevant range when the applicant has ex-
perienced particular emotional difficulties as a result of the event,
and when his or her particular circumstances make the effects
particularly serious. Some of the relevant considerations in relation to this factor are discussed in Sanford v. Koop, 2005 HRTO 53
(CanLII), 2005 HRTO 53 (CanLII) at paras. 34-38.*

Those issues presented in *Sanford v. Koop*,[8] a case involving a complaint of sexual harassment, were as follows:

- *Humiliation experienced by the complainant.*

- *Hurt feelings experienced by the complainant.*

- *A complainant's loss of self-respect.*

- *A complainant's loss of dignity.*

- *A complainant's loss of self-esteem.*

- *A complainant's loss of confidence.*

- *The experience of victimization.*

- *Vulnerability of the complainant.*

- *The seriousness, frequency and duration of the offensive treatment.*

Sanford v. Koop was a pre-amendment decision. It nonetheless remains as an active precedent in the determination of the damage awards
under the revised Code. You should be careful when referring to this case
as it also deals with the former issue of damages for mental anguish when
the conduct was willful, which is no longer applicable.

The damage award should reflect the severity of the circumstances in
question. It was also stated that the loss of long-term employment will
likely be considered more traumatic than newly acquired employment.
The more frequently and hurtful the conduct, the higher the damage
award will likely be.

In Ontario, the damage awards for sexual harassment tend to cluster
in the range of $20,000 to $25,000. The broad spectrum has been noted
to be from $12,000 to $50,000, the award being affected by the factors as
discussed above, whether there was physical touching, the frequency of
the events, and if there was a reprisal.

As summarized in *Garofalo v. Cavalier Hair Stylists Shop Inc.*,[9] a
January 2013 decision of the Tribunal (Bhattacharjee) on the subject of
sexual harassment claims:

*Recent Tribunal decisions that have considered sexual harassment,
sexual solicitations and advances, and/or a poisoned environment*

---

8   *Sanford v. Koop*, 2005, accessed September 2014.
    http://www.canlii.org/en/on/onhrt/doc/2005/2005hrto53/2005hrto53.html
9   *Garofalo v. Cavalier Hair Stylists Shop Inc.*, 2013, accessed September 2014.
    http://www.canlii.org/en/on/onhrt/doc/2013/2013hrto170/2013hrto170.html

based on sex in the context of employment have generally made awards ranging from $12,000 to $50,000 …

[292] In the cases on the low end of the spectrum, the Tribunal generally found that there were few incidents, the incidents were of a less serious nature, and/or the incidents did not include physical touching. In cases on the high end of the spectrum, the Tribunal generally found that there were multiple incidents, the incidents were of a serious nature, there was a serious physical assault, and/or there was a reprisal or a loss of employment related to the incidents.

Apart from these factors, also of influence is the inherent vulnerability of the victim, due to age, economic dependency, or other factors.

The *Smith v. Menzies Chrysler*[10] brought by a male applicant, allowed for a total damage award of $50,000 which was apportioned as $10,000 against two personal respondents individually of $8,000 and $2,000 each, $25,000 against the corporate employer due to a poisoned work environment, and $15,000 for reprisal.

2. The Employer's Response to the Human Rights Complaint

A company which has been served with a human rights complaint should take care to respond to the complaint or letter quickly and diligently.

It has been noted that the manner in which the employer has responded to the claim should be a factor in determining the quantum of the sum to be awarded as compensation. In addition the existence of a harassment policy and its enforcement will also be considered in this context.

The sum to be awarded is not considered as a punitive deterrent, but rather the intent is to make an appropriate compensatory award. The sum is not to be so low as to amount to a licence fee. As was stated in *Payette v. Alarm Guard Security Services:*[11]

Injury to Dignity, Feelings and Self-Respect

[49] It is well established that the Tribunal's remedial powers are not punitive in nature. On the other hand, in assessing quantum, the Tribunal is to be mindful of not setting the amount too low as to effectively create a licensing fee to discriminate.

[50] In Sanford v. Koop, 2005 HRTO 53 (CanLII), 2005 HRTO 53 (CanLII), the Tribunal summarized the factors to be used in assessing the appropriate quantum of damages. They are: humiliation experienced by the complainant; hurt feelings experienced by the complainant; a complainant's loss of self-respect; a complainant's loss of dignity, self-esteem and confidence; the experience of victimization; vulnerability of the complainant; and the seriousness,

---

10 *Smith v. Menzies Chrysler*, 2009, accessed September 2014.
   http://www.canlii.org/en/on/onhrt/doc/2009/2009hrto1936/2009hrto1936.html
11 *Payette v. Alarm Guard Security Services*, 2011, accessed September 2014.
   http://www.canlii.org/en/on/onhrt/doc/2011/2011hrto109/2011hrto109.html

frequency and duration of the offensive treatment. In assessing quantum, the Tribunal is to be mindful of not setting the amount too low thereby trivializing the social importance of the Code and effectively creating a "license fee" to discriminate ...

[51] The Divisional Court has also recognized that humiliation, hurt feelings, the loss of self-respect, dignity and confidence by the applicant, the experience of victimization, the vulnerability of the applicant; and the seriousness of the offensive treatment are among the factors to be considered in setting the amount of damages.

3. Damage Awards in Each Province and Territory

The factors which have been determined to be influential in shaping the sum to be awarded for emotional harm in a sexual harassment case were stated to be as follows in *Torres v. Royalty Kitchenware Ltd.*, (1982), 3 C.H.R.R. D/858 (Ont. Bd. Inq.), a 1982 decision written by Cummings, now Mr. Justice Cummings of the Ontario Superior Court:

1. *The nature of the harassment, that is, was it simply verbal or was it physical as well.*

2. *The degree of aggressiveness and physical contact in the harassment.*

3. *The ongoing nature, that is, the time period of the harassment.*

4. *Its frequency.*

5. *The age of the victim.*

6. *The vulnerability of the victim.*

7. *The psychological impact of the harassment upon the victim.*

As a cautionary note in relying on precedent decisions to set personal damage awards, you should take note that typically awards in sexual harassment cases tend to be higher than in most human rights violations due to the inherent vulnerability of the victims and the likely more severe personal.

If you are presenting a case for sexual harassment, the following are examples of awards made for damages for injured feelings. The awards are all dependent on the facts of each case, which reflect the nature of the offensive conduct and the harm caused to the victim. The cases do illustrate the range, that is, the expected high and low side of the expected recovery.

Awards for injured feelings tend to be provincially/territorially or rather jurisdictionally based. You should focus on precedent cases from within your own jurisdiction, if possible and if not, then use precedent cases from other jurisdictions.

3.1 Ontario examples

In *Hughes v. 1308581 Ontario*,[12] the evidence showed that the personal respondent had pleaded guilty to a charge of criminal harassment, and also had slapped and pinched the complainant's bottom, put his hands under her sweater and touched the lower part of her breasts, as well as he came to her home without invitation and pushed her onto her bed, and tried to grab her inner thigh. The complainant was employed in the position of cashier with a business known as Best Dollar Store, from October 3 to December 9, 2003. An award was made of $25,000 plus lost income.

In *Ratneiya v. Daniel & Krumeh*,[13] the complainant was a student in a law clerk program and was hired by the defendant law firm, the partners of which were a married couple. The Tribunal found that the respondent, Paul Krumeh had sexually harassed the complainant by caressing her lower back, calling her "hairy," asking if her thong was comfortable and told her that it looked good, asked to spank her and did spank her buttocks, and put his arm around her and tried to grab her breast. There was also a finding of reprisal as the complainant's working frequency was altered from one day a week to "on call." A damage award was made of $25,000 plus loss of income.

The complainant in *Payette v. Alarm Guard Services* (see footnote 11 in section **2.**) was employed as a commission sales representative in the Windsor office of the respondent. The personal respondent was her immediate supervisor and was assigned the task of driving her. The complainant's evidence, which was accepted, was that her boss had asked her what kind of underwear she wore, told her when she crossed her arms he could not see her chest, referred to her cotton candy soda pop drink as "cotton panties," offered to take her to a hotel for her birthday, asked her to sit on his lap, said he wanted to jump her, asked her for oral sex, and asked her to sleep with him.

The Tribunal noted that the damage award under the Code is intended to be compensatory and not punitive. The sum awarded should not be so low as to be a licence fee to offend. In this case, the failure of the respondent to effect a timely investigation and to reply to the complaint adversely affected not only her credibility, but also the compensatory award. Even though there was no direct touching in this case, an award of $18,000 was made plus a further sum of $5,000 due to the flawed response to the complaint.

An award of $40,000 was made in *S. H. v. M [...] Painting*[14] in which the offensive conduct was found to be "persistent, unrelenting" and one act of sexual aggression which resulted in a criminal charge.

The same award of $40,000 was made in *Kotevski v. Wimpy's Diner and Krste Petrevski*.[15] The personal respondent told the complainant that

12 *Hughes v. 1308581 Ontario*, 2009, accessed September 2014.
   http://www.canlii.org/en/on/onhrt/doc/2009/2009hrto341/2009hrto341.html
13 *Ratneiya v. Daniel & Krumeh*, 2009, accessed September 2014.
   http://www.canlii.org/en/on/onhrt/doc/2009/2009hrto1824/2009hrto1824.html
14 S. H. v. M [...] Painting, 2009, accessed September 2014.
   http://www.canlii.org/en/on/onhrt/doc/2009/2009hrto595/2009hrto595.html
15 *Kotevski v. Wimpy's Diner and Krste Petrevski*, 2010, accessed September 2014.

he wanted to date her, and asked her out several times, always being declined. Following her pregnancy, during which he paid no attention to the complainant, and after her return to work, Petreveski wrote her letters advising that he loved her, and that he wanted to be with her, even though he was married. In the letters he said he wanted to have sex with her. He left her a note stating that if she did not sleep with him, he would force her to do so.

He also began to touch her in a sexual way, touching her legs, breasts, and buttocks. He frequently tried to enter the bathroom with her. On one occasion, he pushed the bathroom door open and touched her breasts and tried to insert his fingers into her vagina.

On more than one occasion, he masturbated and called the applicant to come and see him. He called her demeaning names and assigned her work which was belittling, such as washing dishes and peeling vegetables, which was not required of other servers.

She sought medical help and was given antidepressants. She suffered from migraines, loss of sleep, and lack of energy. The personal respondent was charged with criminal assault.

It may be noted that no one appeared for the respondents in the liability or remedy hearing. A reconsideration motion was not successful.

3.2 Prince Edward Island example

The Prince Edward Island Human Rights Commission in the case of *Reverend Gael Matheson v. Presbytery of Prince Edward Island*[16] awarded the sum of $50,000 in a complaint which was based on gender discrimination and sexual harassment. The complainant had lost her livelihood as her licence to practice her profession was withheld. The events of adverse treatment took place over an extended time period and her reputation was also damaged by the conduct in question. This is certainly a high award in PEI and elsewhere.

3.3 British Columbia examples

The British Columbia Human Rights Tribunal ordered what had been the highest sum to the date of its publication of $35,000 in *Senyk v. WFG Agency Network (No. 2)* in 2008.[17] This was a case based on discrimination due to a physical and mental disability with respect to an employee of a long-term history.

The range of the expected damage sum for a finding of sexual harassment under the BC legislation can be found in the following passage from the 2008 decision of *Harrison v. Nixon Safety Consulting and others*[18]

http://www.canlii.org/en/on/onhrt/doc/2010/2010hrto1548/2010hrto1548.html
16 *Matheson v. Presbytery of Prince Edward Island*, 2007, accessed September 2014.
   http://www.canlii.org/en/pe/peihrc/doc/2007/2007canlii60951/2007canlii60951.html
17 *Senyk v. WFG Agency Network (No. 2)*, 2008, accessed September 2014.
   http://www.canlii.org/en/bc/bchrt/doc/2008/2008bchrt376/2008bchrt376.html
18 *Harrison v. Nixon Safety Consulting and others*, 2008, accessed September 2014.
   http://www.canlii.org/en/bc/bchrt/doc/2008/2008bchrt462/2008bchrt462.html

The highest award to date for injury to dignity, feelings and self-respect for sexual harassment ($10,000) was made in Gill v. Grammy's Place Restaurant & Bakery Ltd., 2001 BCHRT 33. In Gill, the harassment was extreme and egregious, and not comparable to that in the present case. However, since 2001, damage awards for injury to dignity have risen generally. See, for example, Senyk (No. 2), (para. 470), in which $35,000 was awarded for injury to dignity in a complaint concerning discrimination in employment on the basis of a physical and mental disability, and Datt v. MacDonald's Restaurants of Canada (No. 2), 2006 BCHRT 169 (para. 294), in which $25,000 was awarded for injury to dignity in a complaint concerning discrimination in employment on the basis of a physical disability. In Senyk (No. 2) and Datt, the complainants had been employees of long standing, unlike the situation in the present complaint. As well, the reasons for the large compensatory awards for injury to dignity were distinct from those in the present complaint. While I agree that the nature of the harassment should attract a significant award under this heading, I do not agree that the amount proposed by Ms. Harrison is appropriate. Pursuant to s. 37(2)(d)(iii), I order the respondents, including NSC, to pay Ms. Harrison $15,000 in compensation to her for injury to dignity, feelings and self-respect.

In a recent decision the awarded sum was $12,500 for harassment which was found to be demeaning, provocative, and aggressive, yet without any physical component, in the BC Human Rights Tribunal decision of *McIntosh v. Metro Aluminum Products:*[19]

In this case, the harassment is in written form, consisting of unwelcome sexual propositions and sexually demeaning language. In that respect, it is more analogous to sexual harassment of a verbal nature, though I note that whether verbal, written or physical, sexual harassment of any kind can adversely and significantly affect a person's dignity and self-respect. In this case, I find that Mr. Augustynowicz's repeated sexual comments were of a serious nature. The texts were aggressive in tone, provocative and demeaning.

[154] Ms. McIntosh testified, and I accept, that the sexual harassment was occurring regularly between late June to September 22. As noted earlier, while there is no record of any texts in August, I accept Ms. McIntosh's evidence that there were texts of a similar nature occurring during that time. The sexual harassment was not an isolated incident, or one or two comments, but was frequent, repetitive and particularly offensive. As well, Mr. Augustynowicz continued to send the messages after being advised they were unwelcome on more than one occasion, which makes his conduct more egregious.

[155] Ms. McIntosh's age is a relatively neutral factor which does not serve to increase or decrease any damage award.

19 *McIntosh v. Metro Aluminum Products and another*, 2011, accessed September 2014.
http://www.canlii.org/en/bc/bchrt/doc/2011/2011bchrt34/2011bchrt34.html

[156] I find that Ms. McIntosh was particularly vulnerable given the power imbalance between her and Mr. Augustynowicz, her reliance on her employment to support herself, and her medical condition. The Respondents say that there is no evidence connecting the texting to her colitis or any other physical or emotional ailment. They say that her demeanour and stress level may have changed due to an aggravation of her colitis caused by other factors, such as the termination of the sexual relationship with Mr. Augustynowicz, which is not the subject of the complaint before the Tribunal. As they note, "not every affair has a happy ending, and ending a relationship can be traumatic. Who is to say the cause of the complainant's unhappiness?"

[157] I accept, and have taken into consideration in my assessment of damages under this heading, that there was most probably some physical and emotional impact arising out of the end of the consensual relationship. I also accept Ms. McIntosh's evidence that the incessant, sexually harassing texting after the relationship ended made her "feel like garbage" and made her working life very difficult to endure. She testified the stress became overwhelming and that she was "almost on the verge having a nervous breakdown" in September. Ms. McIntosh was still in obvious emotional upset as she gave her evidence. It was apparent that there was a continuing impact on her, which included impact arising out of the sexual harassment.

[158] Ms. McIntosh also provided medical notes, one of which attested to "work related stress" requiring a significant period off work, as well as a medical note referring to an ongoing problem with ulcerative colitis in December 2008.

[159] Taking into consideration Ms. McIntosh's evidence, the medical information and Mrs. Perrin's observations of her daughter during the summer and fall of 2008, I am satisfied that there was a significant and ongoing physical and emotional impact of the sexual harassment on Ms. McIntosh.

[160] I have also considered the fact that the sexual harassment was at the core of Ms. McIntosh's departure from the workplace.

[161] After considering all of the above circumstances, I exercise my discretion pursuant to s. 37(2)(d)(iii) to award $12,500 to Ms. McIntosh as damages for injury to dignity, feelings and self-respect.

3.4 Nova Scotia examples

The 2007 decision of the Board of Inquiry in *Couttreau v. R. Ellis Chevrolet Oldsmobile Limited*[20] provides a good review of the range of likely damage awards for this province. The submission was made and rejected that there was a high water mark of $10,000 for this type of remedy. The

20 *Couttreau v. R. Ellis Chevrolet Oldsmobile Limited*, 2007, accessed September 2014.
   http://www.canlii.org/en/ns/nshrc/doc/2007/2007nshrc3/2007nshrc3.html

Board noted that the sum awarded should reflect the serious nature of adverse treatment under the Code and that harm to a person's self-worth is destructive and takes a longer time to heal than a minor physical ailment.

In this case, Couttreau was adversely treated due to a physical disability. He was able to find other employment in four months after his dismissal, although at a lesser salary. He showed no direct evidence of long-term psychological damage or injury to his self-worth. He was awarded $10,000.

In the *Cromwell v. Leon's Furniture Limited*[21] case, the Board awarded $8,000 after finding a violation of the Code, also due to a disability. The award seems low in view of its findings below. The Board did note that there was no medical evidence introduced. It spoke as follows:

> In the circumstances of this case, the discrimination resulted in long-term injury to the Complainant's self-worth. The financial and emotional stability of the Complainant's life was significantly impacted and thrown off course as a result of the discrimination she experienced. The Complainant had to declare bankruptcy, was required to move her family and eventually took a lengthy medical leave alleged to be stress-related. While the Respondent cannot be held legally responsible for these subsequent events, there is no doubt that the Complainant's dignity was impacted, that she suffered a loss of self-respect and her sense of personal security and stability underwent significant upheaval by virtue of the effect of the discrimination upon her. I have also taken into consideration the nature of the discriminatory experience and the Respondent's response to the complaint. I conclude that it is appropriate to award the Complainant $8,000.00 in general damages for the discrimination that she experienced while employed with the Respondent. Accordingly, it is ordered that, within 30 days of the date of this decision, the Respondent shall pay the Complainant damages in the amount of $8,000.00.

The leading case in Nova Scotia, the decision of *Hill v. Misener (No. 2)* (1997) CHRR Doc 97-215 described the concept of the damage award in these words:

> In a physical injury, damages in the range of $2,000, to represent an extremely minor physical problem which resolves quickly. People who sustain minor physical injuries do not question who they are, they do not question their self-worth, they do not question their value as human beings. An injury to one's self-respect, dignity and self-worth is an injury that is far more destructive and painful and takes a longer time to heal than a minor physical injury.
>
> General damage awards which have not properly applied the compensatory principles do not reflect the serious nature of discrimination and fail horribly to uphold the principles which have been established by Human Rights Legislation.

---

21 *Cromwell v. Leon's Furniture Limited*, 2014, accessed September 2014.
http://www.canlii.org/en/ns/nshrc/doc/2014/2014canlii16399/2014canlii16399.html

No award was made in this case, although an assessment was made of $15,000. No case in Nova Scotia has made an equivalent award.

One reason for the range of damage awards being modest is that the complainant often fails to bring forward medical evidence to demonstrate the consequences caused by the adverse conduct. This was noted by the Board in *Davison v. Nova Scotia Construction Safety Association.*[22]

> *I am shocked when reading human rights decisions at how rarely evidence of the sort submitted to the tribunal in Miller v. Sam's Pizza House is put in evidence in human rights cases. In most such cases, including this one, the evidence introduced by counsel for the Commission on behalf of the complainant (who usually does not have a lawyer of his or her own) is limited to brief testimony by the Complainant about the impact of the discrimination on him or her, with no introduction, for example, of medical testimony with respect to the physical and mental health consequences that discrimination may have on a complainant. This is unfortunate, because there is a growing body of evidence that the health impact of discrimination on its targets can be quite severe. See, for example, see S.A. Lenhart, Clinical Aspects of Sexual Harassment and Gender Discrimination: Psychological Consequences and Treatment Interventions (Brunner-Routledge, 2004), where the author states at p. 135 of her text:*

> *A large number of physical symptoms have been reported in relation to discriminatory experiences, including gastrointestinal disorders, jaw tightening, teeth grinding, dizziness, nausea, diarrhea, tics, muscle spasms, fatigue, dyspepsia, neck pain, back pain, pulse changes, headaches, weight loss, weight gain, increased perspiration, cold feet and hands, loss of appetite, binge eating, decreased libido, delayed recovery from illness, sleep disruption, increased respiratory or urinary tract infections, recurrences of chronic illnesses, ulcers, irritable bowel syndrome, migraines, eczema, and urticaria. ...Psychological reactions that have been reported include persistent sadness, negative outlook, irritability, lability, anergia and hypergia, mood swings, impulsivity, emotional flooding, anxiety, fears of loss of control, excessive guilt and shame, escape fantasies, compulsive thoughts, rage episodes, obsessional fears, crying spells, persistent anger and fear, decreased self-esteem, self-doubt, diminished self-confidence, decreased concentration, anhedonia, and feelings of humiliation, helplessness, vulnerability, and alienation. The psychiatric disorders that have been reported include 1) anxiety disorders, especially generalized anxiety disorder, post-traumatic stress disorder, acute stress disorder, and dissociation disorders; (2) somatization disorders; (3) sleep disorders; (4) sexual function disorders; (5) psychoactive substance abuse disorders; (6) depressive disorders; and (8) DSM-IV ...V code diagnoses associated with marital, occupational, interpersonal and bereavement issues.*

---

22 *Davison v. Nova Scotia Construction Safety Association*, 2005, accessed September 2014. http://www.canlii.org/en/ns/nshrc/doc/2005/2005nshrc4/2005nshrc4.html

[391] I would encourage Commission counsel or other lawyers rep-
resenting Complainants in future human rights cases with respect
to damage claims, to explore with Complainants the presence or
absence of the broad range of symptoms described above, to bring
out evidence of such symptoms during the testimony of the Com-
plainant if they in fact exist, and to consider providing expert testi-
mony to assist Boards of Inquiry in making accurate and adequate
awards of general damages. I suspect that the absence of such tes-
timony is one of the reasons that awards of general damages in
human rights cases have historically been so low.

3.5 New Brunswick examples

The recent decision of the Labour and Employment Board in *Downey
v. Keenan Truck Repair Inc.*[23] also found against the complainant, but
similarly made a provisional damage award, in this instance in the sum
of $17,500. The complaint was based on a physical disability, carpal tun-
nel syndrome. The Board noted that the assessment of the general damage
award should be based on the following factors:

> *Considerations reflected in the general damage award are humili-
> ation, hurt feelings, loss of dignity and self-respect, vulnerability
> of the claimant and "the seriousness, frequency and duration of
> the offensive treatment." See Ketola v. Value Propane Inc., [2002]
> O.H.R.B.I.D. No. 14 at para. 14.*

In this instance, although age was not advanced as a ground of the
complaint, it was considered as a factor in determining the award, likely as
it added to the vulnerability of the complainant, as it was described to be
"an aggravating factor." He was 63 years of age when he was terminated.

An award of $15,000 for general damages was made in the Board deci-
sion of *S. W. E. v. B. K.*,[24] in which there was a finding of sexual harassment
over a nine-month period and a sexual assault, conduct which required
psychological counseling.

3.6 Newfoundland and Labrador examples

The Supreme Court of Newfoundland and Labrador in *St. John's (City) v.
Human Rights Commission*[25] set aside the finding of liability made at the
human rights inquiry, a case which was based on a mental disability. An
award of $20,000 had been made at the first hearing; however, the court
considered this award overly generous and set the sum at $7,500.

Awards tend to be modest. The complainant in *MacDonald v. Dental
and Hearing Crafts Ltd.*[26] was found to have been terminated unfairly due
to a mental disability and was awarded $4,000.

23 *Downey v. Keenan Truck Repair Inc.*, 2014, accessed September 2014.
    http://www.canlii.org/en/nb/nbleb/doc/2014/2014canlii9593/2014canlii9593.html
24 *S. W. E. v. B. K.*, 2007, accessed September 2014.
    http://www.canlii.org/en/nb/nbleb/doc/2007/2007canlii37872/2007canlii37872.html
25 *St. John's (City) v. Human Rights Commission*, 2011, accessed September 2014.
    http://www.canlii.org/en/nl/nlsctd/doc/2011/2011nltd83/2011nltd83.html
26 *MacDonald v. Dental and Hearing Crafts Ltd.*, 2009, accessed September 2014.
    http://www.canlii.org/en/nl/nlhrc/doc/2009/2009canlii85611/2009canlii85611.html

3.7 Manitoba examples

In *K. K. v. Hair Passion*,[27] the Manitoba Board made a finding that the complainant had been terminated due to her mental disability (bipolar depression) and while it made findings of the impact of this on the complainant, as noted below, the award made was the relatively insignificant sum of $2,000:

> *I am satisfied that while the personal relationship was very important to the Complainant, the employment itself was also important to her, and that the termination of her employment would have had, and did have, a significant impact on her sense of identity and self-respect.*

Reflective of the range of damage awards to be expected is the submission made by the Human Rights Commission in *CR v. Canadian Mental Health Association*:[28]

> *The Commission conceded that its request in this case for $6,000 in general damages was high, but highlighted the facts that the Respondent is an organization which deals with and employs a large number of individuals who have disabilities, and that the Respondent's reliance on what the Commission submitted was a fabricated pretext for the Complainant's dismissal only served to further hinder her future employment prospects.*

In this case, the finding was made that the breach was serious, the victim was vulnerable, and that she was threatened with probation and suspension, and then termination followed. The sum of $4,000 was awarded. This seems inordinately modest, in my view.

3.8 Saskatchewan example

The Saskatchewan jurisdiction remains the only forum with a statutory ceiling for the damage sum to be awarded, which is capped at $10,000. An example of a decision noting the ceiling, which was then set at $5,000 is *Saskatchewan (Human Rights Commission) v. Country Leathers Manufacturing Ltd.*[29]

The Board has authority to order additional damages where the company's conduct is willful and reckless, although both sums are subject to the total cap of $10,000. Why this is so is beyond belief. A maximum sum set for an award of compensatory damages in this modest amount surely fits into the realm of a licence fee, in my mind, given a comparison to the sums awarded in other jurisdictions.

---

27 *K. K. v. Hair Passion*, 2013, accessed September 2014.
   http://www.canlii.org/en/mb/mbhrc/doc/2013/2013canlii3982/2013canlii3982.html
28 *CR v. Canadian Mental Health Association, Westman Region Inc.*, 2013, accessed September 2014.
   http://www.canlii.org/en/mb/mbhrc/doc/2013/2013canlii125/2013canlii125.html
29 *Saskatchewan (Human Rights Commission) v. Country Leathers Manufacturing Ltd.*, 2004, accessed
   September 2014. http://www.canlii.org/en/sk/skca/doc/2004/2004skca156/2004skca156.html

3.9 Alberta examples

The recent damage awards in Alberta have become comparatively generous. In the case of *Walsh v. Mobil Oil Canada*,[30] the case was based on adverse treatment due to gender. A second complaint was made based on reprisal. The Human Rights Tribunal awarded $10,000 and $25,000 respectively for general damages. Professional medical evidence was used to support the claim. These sums are comparatively high.

The award was reviewed and upheld. The Alberta Court of Queen's Bench stated:

> *[126] It is quite true that there is no precedent for a $25,000 award for a single complaint under the Act or any of its predecessors in Alberta law. That, however, is no basis for interfering with Ms. Bryant's conclusions. The Act sets no limits. Further, the compensatory nature of the Act which is the basis for the use of tort principles in assessing compensation suggests that tort law could provide guidance on quantum of damages payable in case of psychological injury. Ms. Bryant accepted medical opinion that Ms. Walsh suffered a stress disorder, brought about by the circumstances of her employment, and recognized comments of Macleod, J. in describing the insensitivity and cruelty of Mobil's retaliatory actions in contributing to this stress disorder. In light of the fact that a psychological injury in tort can give rise to non-pecuniary damage awards in the range of $40,000 and up, I find there is nothing untoward in the sum of $25,000 as selected by Ms. Bryant.*

This decision was upheld in the Alberta Court of Appeal.[31]

The Board noted in *Chieriro v. Michetti*[32] that the damages suffered by the victim in employment cases are distinct:

> *When an employer discriminates, and such discrimination is a factor in the loss of employment, an award which appropriately recognizes the emotional harm associated with the loss of this most important facet in a person's life is warranted. Compensation here is completely separate from any wage loss claim and is awarded to compensate for the intrinsic harm connected to the distress experienced during and even after employment recovery. As here, such harm does not necessarily end when a replacement job and income are secured. When a job ending stems in part from a protected ground, it has potential to strike at the very core of a person, a core that human rights legislation is intended to protect. This harm may not amount to a full blown psychological injury as existed in Walsh, supra, but is compensable nonetheless. In human rights the aim of damages is remedial; to make the victim whole or restore the victim of discrimination to the position he would have*

30 *Walsh v. Mobil Oil Canada, (Exxmobil Canada Ltd.)*, 2012, accessed September 2014.
   http://www.canlii.org/en/ab/abqb/doc/2012/2012abqb527/2012abqb527.html
31 *Walsh v. Mobil Oil Canada*, 2013 (Court of Appeal of Alberta decision), accessed September 2014.
   http://www.canlii.org/en/ab/abca/doc/2013/2013abca238/2013abca238.html
32 *Chieriro v. Michetti*, 2013, accessed September 2014.
   http://www.canlii.org/en/ab/abhrc/doc/2013/2013ahrc3/2013ahrc3.html

been in but for the discrimination. In this case, real injuries and harm associated with the loss of, and Mr. Chieriro's subsequent need, to recover employment were established and persisted, quite separate from wage loss.

To the same end is a similar decision of the Alberta Tribunal in *Cowling v. Her Majesty the Queen in Right of Alberta as represented by Alberta Employment and Immigration*[33] in which the Board stated a fair award would be set at $15,000 in a case based on age discrimination:

> *In her testimony Ms. Cowling explained the grief, loss of dignity and self-esteem she experienced following her release from Mediation Services, her difficult search for employment and the discrimination attached to her circumstances because of her age. In her testimony, Ms. Cowling made it clear that the impact of being unemployed and refused employment in the Alberta branch she had successfully worked in for eight years was humiliating and devastating for her.*
>
> *[235] In Arunachalam v. Best Buy Canada Ltd.,[7] the Ontario Human Rights Tribunal spoke about the importance of acknowledging injuries which are not related to financial losses but that are, nonetheless important to recognize because of the immeasurable harm that is cast on a complainant emotionally and psychologically.*
>
> *[236] In the decision, Jonathan Simpson v. Oil City Hospitality Group Inc., 1260055 Alberta Limited operating as Oil City Roadhouse,[8] Tribunal member McFetridge stated, with regard to potential general damages awarded in cases of injury to dignity, that the "consequences of the respondent's violation of the Act should be recognized though a significant award of general damages."*
>
> *[237] I also subscribe to Tribunal member McFetridge's determination that injury to dignity and all that encompasses, should be compensated in a manner that will provide "real redress to the complainant and encourage respect for the principles set out in the legislation."*
>
> *[238] Considering all that Ms. Cowling was subjected to by her employer during the final years of her employment in Alberta's Mediation Services, an award of $15,000.00 is appropriate for the significant injury to Ms. Cowling's dignity and self-esteem.*

The case of *Carriere v. Boonstra Trucking Ltd (BTL)*.[34] resulted in an award of $15,000. The complainant had injured himself in a slip-and-fall accident and was terminated following his return to work. The Board noted:

> *I accept that Mr. Carriere's termination of employment from BTL impacted him financially and caused injury to dignity and self-*

---

33 *Alberta Tribunal in Cowling v. Her Majesty the Queen in Right of Alberta as represented by Alberta Employment and Immigration,* 2012, accessed September 2014.
http://www.canlii.org/en/ab/abhrc/doc/2012/2012ahrc12/2012ahrc12.html
34 *Carriere v. Boonstra Trucking Ltd.,* 2013, accessed September 2014.
http://www.canlii.org/en/ab/abhrc/doc/2013/2013ahrc10/2013ahrc10.html

respect. Mr. Carriere stated that he wanted to make a good im-
pression and tried his best in his work for BTL. The termination
made him feel hurt, useless and worthless. He felt that despite giv-
ing all he could offer to the job he was made to feel he had nothing
more to contribute and he had given up.

3.10 Nunavut example

An award of $10,000 was made in the decision of the Nunavut Human
Rights Tribunal decision of *Petaulassie v. Hamlet of Cape Dorset.*[35] The
claim was based on family status. The Tribunal defined the loss based on
the following:

Mr. Petaulassie is asking for $10,000.00 for injury to dignity and
self-respect as a result of the discrimination. This type of award
is commonly used in human rights cases where discrimination or
harassment has been found to have occurred to compensate the
applicant for the loss of the right to be free from discrimination.
This includes compensation for the humiliation, injury to dignity
and self-respect, and emotional harm that results from the dis-
crimination. Mr. Petaulassie described the impact on him of losing
an opportunity to be employed by the Hamlet and remain in his
community. He stated, and I accept, that the impact of learning
that a family member had been preferred over him and that he
could not remain and work in his own community made him feel
"sick to his stomach" and had a significant impact on him.

3.11 Northwest Territories example

An award of $25,000 was made in *Thorson v. The Government of the*
Northwest Territories[36] by the Human Rights Panel in 2013. This is the
highest award in the NWT jurisdiction to date. The complaint was based
on adverse treatment due to depression and was influenced by the egregious conduct of the employer, the 18-month time period over which the
conduct took place, threats of termination and the failure to accommodate
the complainant and the harm suffered by her.

3.12 Yukon examples

A recent decision of the Yukon Human Rights Board found that there had
been conduct which was sexual harassment. However, it ordered no compensatory damages. The conduct in question involved minimal physical
contact. The Supreme Court of Yukon set aside this decision in *Hureau v.*
Yukon Human Rights Board of Adjudication[37] and allowed an award in
the sum of $5,000, in addition to the initial award of three months com-
pensation for lost income. The complainant was young and was employed
in her first position.

35 *Petaulassie v. Hamlet of Cape Dorset*, 2012, accessed September 2014.
   http://www.canlii.org/en/nu/nuhrt/doc/2012/2012nhrt2/2012nhrt2.html
36 *Thorson v. The Government of the Northwest Territories*, 2013, accessed September 2014.
   http://www.canlii.org/en/nt/nthrap/doc/2013/2013canlii82655/2013canlii82655.html
37 *Hureau v. Yukon Human Rights Board of Adjudication*, 2014, accessed September 2014.
   http://www.canlii.org/en/yk/yksc/doc/2014/2014yksc21/2014yksc21.html

The Court agreed with an earlier Prince Edward Island decision of *MacTavish v. Government of Prince Edward Island*,[38] which stated:

> General damages in human rights cases are not intended to punish the wrongdoer. They reflect a recognition by society that one has been harmed by the actions of another. The harm we speak of with respect to general damages in these cases is not monetary harm. It is harm to the dignity and self-respect of the victim. We must attempt to restore, but not reward. We must be realistic and consider whether any award bears a reasonable relationship to other awards for similar discrimination.

3.13 Quebec example

A claim for a human rights violation will lead to an award of moral damages. The general description of the qualifying principles is set out as follows in *Québec (Commission des droits de la personne et des droits de la jeunesse) v. Centre maraîcher Eugène Guinois JR Inc.*[39] Awards were made to each complainant in the sum of $10,000 each due to adverse treatment due to race.

> [217] It is always difficult to assess moral damages, given that the prejudice sustained is evaluated on a purely subjective basis. There is no visible injury, although the injury is no less real.
>
> Although it is less palpable, it is no less real:[27]
>
> Moral or extrapatrimonial damage is often difficult to quantify precisely or even approximately. … In all these cases, however, the prejudice is direct, definite and real, and must therefore be compensated for, even if there is no scientific basis for assessing it precisely.
>
> Although moral prejudice is more difficult to define, that in no way diminishes the injury it constitutes. I would go so far as to say that moral prejudice is all the more pernicious because it is not apparent. It affects a human being deep down inside, in the ramifications for his or her personal nature, and destroys the serenity to which he or she aspires. It attacks his or her dignity and leaves the individual shaken, alone in fighting the effects of an evil he or she carries inside rather than on his or her person or property.[28]
>
> [219] The Honourable Sheehan J. of this Tribunal wrote the following:
>
> > It is well known that the victims of harassment agree to bear, and endure as best they can, a situation that is constraining and degrading. That is easily understood in regard to employees who, like us all, are experiencing economic difficulties. That is particularly true in the framework of a hierarchical relationship. There

---

38 *MacTavish v. Government of Prince Edward Island*, 2009, accessed September 2014.
   http://www.canlii.org/en/pe/pesctd/doc/2009/2009pesc18/2009pesc18.html
39 *Québec (Commission des droits de la personne et des droits de la jeunesse) v. Centre maraîcher Eugène Guinois JR Inc.*, 2005, accessed September 2014.
   http://www.canlii.org/en/qc/qctdp/doc/2005/2005canlii11754/2005canlii11754.html

is no "proper" or "improper," or even "incompatible," conduct for a victim of discrimination and sexual harassment.[29]

3.14 Federal legislation example

The federal legislation has been interpreted to allow for damage claims on similar principles. An example of a recent award is that of *Johnstone v. Canada Border Service Agency (CBSA)*[40] in which $15,000 was ordered to compensate for adverse treatment due to family status. There is a maximum set by the Act at $20,000 for pain and suffering.

Canadian Human Rights Act also allows for an increased damage award of "special compensation" up to a further sum of $20,000 when the conduct in question is willful and malicious. In this case, such an incremental award was also made:

> *This Tribunal finds that CBSA, by ignoring so many efforts both externally and internally to bring about change with respect to its family status policies of accommodation has deliberately denied protection to those in need of it.*
>
> *[381] CBSA, and its organizational predecessor's lack of effort and lack of concern takes many forms over many years including: disregard for the Brown decision after writing a letter of apology; developing a model policy and then burying it (some management knew of it, some did not); pursuing arbitrary policies that are unwritten and not universally followed; lack of human rights awareness training even at the senior management level; the proffering of a floodgates argument 5 years after the complaint with the Respondent giving insufficient time and data to its own expert to enable him to provide a helpful expert opinion; and no attempt to inquire of Ms. Johnstone as to her particular circumstances or inform her of options to meet her needs.*
>
> *[382] Given all the circumstances of this case, this Tribunal awards Ms. Johnstone $20,000.00 under this heading. CBSA's conduct has been willful and reckless, showing a disregard for Ms. Johnstone's situation and denying that a duty to accommodate exists on grounds of family status arising for childcare responsibilities such as hers.*

The Federal Court upheld this decision,[41] which itself was appealed unsuccessfully on this issue to the Federal Court of Appeal.[42]

4. Punitive Damages

Punitive damages are considered damages that go beyond simple compensation and are awarded to punish the defendant. The *Canadian Human*

---

40 *Johnstone v. Canada Border Service Agency*, 2010, accessed September 2014.
    http://www.canlii.org/en/ca/chrt/doc/2010/2010chrt20/2010chrt20.html
41 *Canada (Attorney General) v. Johnstone*, 2013 (decision upheld), accessed September 2014.
    http://www.canlii.org/en/ca/fct/doc/2013/2013fc113/2013fc113.html
42 *Canada (Attorney General) v. Johnstone*, 2013 (appeal unsuccessful), accessed September 2014.
    http://www.canlii.org/en/ca/fca/doc/2014/2014fca110/2014fca110.html

Rights Act does not use the precise vocabulary of "punitive damages" but the Act allows for an increased damage award of "special compensation" up to a further sum of $20,000 when the conduct in question is willful and malicious. Note that awards of punitive damages remain rare.

The Charter in Quebec allows for an award of punitive damages where the conduct is reckless, that is, a standard less than intentional. Such conduct was found resulting in an award of $5,000 each for incremental punitive damages. An award of $50,000 in punitive damages and $25,000 in moral damages was ordered against Bombardier for failing to hire a Muslim pilot.

Manitoba allows for punitive damages where the questioned conduct shows malice or recklessness up to $5,000 and $25,000 against an individual or corporation respectively. The Yukon also provides the same remedy.

The Northwest Territories allows for punitive damages up to a cap of $10,000.

Nunavut has no set maximum but its statute allows for such incremental damages where the conduct again shows malice or reckless behaviour.

Saskatchewan's statute allows for an incremental award where the conduct is proven as reckless. The compensatory sum and this incremental award are capped at a total of $10,000 in tandem.

Ontario's statute has no such provision. Punitive damages are not now awarded in Ontario. This is also the case in in the Atlantic provinces, British Columbia, and Alberta.

5. Costs

Costs include more than just lawyer's fees. Costs may include expert fees, travel costs, office expenses, and much more. When the trial has concluded, the judge may order the losing party to pay a portion of the winning party's costs. The Court makes the decision on whether or not costs are awarded and how much the winning party receives.

The Supreme Court of Canada has determined that the relevant statute must specifically allow for an order of costs, failing which the residual authority of the remedy section of the code in question cannot be used to allow for such an award.

Here are some examples:

- *Quebec's Charter allows for a costs award in favour of the Commission.*

- *Newfoundland's statute allows for "costs as appropriate."*

- *Yukon allows for a costs award.*

- *Nunavut's statute provides authority for such an award where the claim has been "knowingly false," or if the investigation has been unduly hampered by the conduct of either party. This presumably does not require a liability finding on the substantive complaint.*

- *BC's Act provides for a costs award where there has been "improper conduct."*

7
Reinstatement Remedies

1. Special Damages: Lost Income

You may claim for "special damages" or lost income where you have been directly or constructively terminated due to a human rights violation or reprisal.

You can also assert a termination as a reprisal against a complaint or threatened complaint, which is independent of a finding of a breach of the human rights code substantive violation. Some jurisdictions require an actual complaint be filed before a reprisal remedy is allowed, which is discussed below.

1.1 Principle of "make whole"

You must appreciate the differences between a wrongful dismissal case and a human rights case. In a human rights claim, the length of the complainant's employment history and the nature of the position held by him or her does not impact on how the lost income claim is determined. This is due to the remedy in a human rights case to "make whole" the victim from the loss of employment.

You will need an example of case law to show that this concept is the accepted standard of determining the claim for lost income. If you are arguing a human rights lost income claim in any jurisdiction, this concept applies.

The following awards are reflective of the approach taken in human rights cases. This method of determining the income loss to be paid to the victim is remarkably different from the analysis in the wrongful dismissal cases, which is dependent on the length of the employment relationship and the nature of the position held to determine the "period of notice" which becomes the maximum sum of lost income to be awarded. There is no such cap in human rights cases. The following are summaries of precedent cases that can be used to establish this principle:

- *In Airport Taxicab (Malton) Assn. v. Piazza (1989), the Ontario Court of Appeal upheld the award of the Board of Inquiry (Zemans) award of 11 weeks' lost income after 10 weeks of employment in the sum of $2,750. This amount represented the complainant's period of unemployment subsequent to her termination and hence was a "make whole" remedy. The Divisional Court, on the first appeal, had previously reduced the damages for lost wages to $750.*

  In the Piazza decision, the Court of Appeal, in reversing the Divisional Court, applied the "make whole" concept and confirmed that under human rights legislation, the purpose of compensation is to restore the complainant to the prior position that she "would have been in had the discriminatory [conduct] not occurred."

- *In 1998 in Ontario Human Rights Commission v. Impact Interiors Inc.,[1] in a reversal of a first-level appeal decision of the Divisional Court, the Ontario Court of Appeal ruled the remedy under the Code is restitutional (i.e., make whole) in nature and hence the length of employment and the "quality" of the position held, which presumably means the type of position, are both irrelevant factors in the assessment of the income loss.*

  In this case the complainant, Cindy Petersen, had been employed for two days, at which time she ceased her employment due to the sexual harassing conduct of the employer. The Board of Inquiry ordered a lost wage claim of $17,272, which represented the difference between what she would have earned in her former job and what she actually earned from her last date of active employment to the date of the hearing, a time period of two years and eighteen weeks. The Divisional Court had improperly reduced the award in favour of Ms. Peterson to $7,500, based on the theory that there must be some relation between the award of lost wages and the length and quality of the complainant's prior position.

  The second complainant, Shirley Hom, was a student who had been employed for five days. She was awarded lost compensation from the date of last active employment on June 10 through to the date of her return to school on September 10, 1990.

You need to be aware of the limitations on this manner of determining the income loss. You must prove that the lost income claim was caused

1 *Ontario Human Rights Commission v. Impact Interiors Inc.*, 1998, accessed September 2014. http://www.canlii.org/en/on/onca/doc/1998/1998canlii17685/1998canlii17685.html

by the wrongdoing. This is called the "causation" factor. Essentially this means that there are no other intervening factors which may have caused the lost income claim to continue.

An employer may argue that you have failed in a duty to "mitigate" or seek new employment. If this argument succeeds, the claim would be reduced based on the new income which could have been earned. You need to show evidence of your job search to demonstrate that you have been active in looking for other employment.

In the case of *Walsh v. Mobil Oil Canada*,[2] in which the Tribunal had found that the complainant's unemployment was caused by the conduct of the employer for five years until 2000 and thereafter the claim for lost income was not allowed as other forces had intervened. It was determined that the applicant's medical condition made her unable to work from 2000 forward. This decision was upheld in the Court of Appeal.

A lost income claim was allowed in *Hughes v. 1308581 Ontario*.[3] The complainant had been employed for approximately two months. She was terminated as a cashier on December 9, 2003. The lost income claim was allowed to January 31, 2004, such being the date the business closed.

The argument was made by the employee that she was unable to work due to the emotional trauma to that date and beyond. This was not successful as the application of the "but-for test" (i.e., but for the action the result would not have happened) meant that her employment would have ceased with the closing of the business.

It was decided that the lost income claim was limited by the closing of the company's business. In the application of the make-whole concept of the determination of the damage award, the real life circumstance of the employer's business had to be considered and applied.

Here are some more cases dealing with the make whole concept of defining the income loss that you can use in a hearing or settlement conference to make your lost income claim.

The analysis to determine the lost income claim in a human rights case is summarized in the decision of the Ontario Human Rights Tribunal in the case of *Chittle v. 1056263 Ontario*:[4]

> *Pursuant to subsection 45.2 (1), above, an applicant who proves a breach of section 5 of the Code is entitled to compensation for wage loss arising out of the discriminatory act. Subsection 45.2 (1)1 of the Code directs the Tribunal to consider what loss arose "out of the infringement" of the Code when considering the proper amount of monetary compensation. In Airport Taxicab (Malton) Assn. v. Piazza, (1989), 10 C.H.R.R. D/6347 (Ont. C.A.), the Ontario Court of Appeal at para. 45017, stated that the "purpose of the compensation*

2   *Walsh v. Mobil Oil Canada*, 2013, accessed September 2014.
    http://www.canlii.org/en/ab/abca/doc/2013/2013abca238/2013abca238.html
3   *Hughes v. 1308581 Ontario*, 2009, accessed September 2014.
    http://www.canlii.org/en/on/onhrt/doc/2009/2009hrto341/2009hrto341.html
4   *Chittle v. 1056263 Ontario*, 2013, accessed September 2014.
    http://www.canlii.org/en/on/onhrt/doc/2013/2013hrto1261/2013hrto1261.html

is to restore a complainant as far as is reasonably possible to the position that the complainant would have been in had the discriminatory act not occurred." Decisions of this Tribunal and of its predecessor Boards of Inquiry have commonly considered loss arising from the date of the infringement of the Code to the date of the hearing, (although there has been some discussion of awards and one actual award for wage loss going beyond the date of the hearing ... The amount is reduced to account for any employment income received during the period, and may be reduced for other reasons, such as evidence that the applicant's employment would have been reduced or eliminated for reasons unrelated to a breach of the Code.

A similar view was taken by the Alberta Human Rights Tribunal in the March 2012 decision in *Schulz v. Lethbridge Industries Limited*[5] in determining the appropriate income loss for a case which took five and a half years to reach hearing. The claim was based on physical and mental issues. The decision noted the make whole concept but declined to make any finding of fault on either party as to delay or even to assess whether it was systemic in awarding an income loss of 30 months. It was also noted that reinstatement was not requested. The reduction in the award appeared to be due to the risk that had Mr. Schulz been returned to work earlier, he would not have medically been able to fulfill the requirements of the position.

A similar finding was made in the decision of the Canadian Human Rights Tribunal decision in *Milano v. Triple K Transport Ltd.*[6] in which the lost income claim was reduced due to the evidence offered by the employer that it was required to reduce its labour force in the time period following termination; hence the employee would likely have been terminated in this time period, even had there not been a human rights violation.

Whether the claim is based on a direct termination or a lost opportunity, it is clear that the lost income claim must satisfy the first criterion of a causal link. The Alberta Court of Appeal in *Walsh v. Mobil Oil Canada* (see footnote 2) stated that "there must be a causal link between the discriminatory practice and the loss claimed."

The causal link, as determined by the appellate court in *Walsh* was the "but-for test." To reiterate, this test means: But for the employer's adverse conduct, what income would have the applicant otherwise have earned?

In *Walsh* itself, the Court of Appeal agreed with the Tribunal's decision that the claim did initially satisfy this test, but five years following the violation, other factors had intervened to extinguish the causal link.

These cases conclude that the lost income claim is based on the test set out above, but for the employer's adverse conduct, what income would have otherwise been earned? Such a test would look to the adverse conduct

---

5   *Schulz v. Lethbridge Industries Limited*, 2012, accessed September 2014.
    http://www.canlii.org/en/ab/abhrc/doc/2012/2012ahrc3/2012ahrc3.html
6   *Milano v. Triple K Transport Ltd.*, 2003, accessed September 2014.
    http://www.canlii.org/en/ca/chrt/doc/2003/2003chrt30/2003chrt30.html#par66

and determine if the loss of income is caused by such conduct. A termination, direct or constructive, caused by discriminatory conduct, would fit this test.

What all this really means is that when applying the but-for test, you need to prove that your lost income resulted from the unfair human rights violation of the company and that the continued loss was not due to any intervening factors which were unrelated to the initial termination decision.

The Alberta Court of Appeal in *Walsh v. Mobil Oil Canada* agreed with the concept of the make whole remedy for the determination of the income loss and then questioned what limits or restrictions should be applied on this loss. This was in the context of reviewing an award made by the Tribunal for an income loss of some magnitude of $472,000, representing a five-year period, yet which fell short of the full income loss sought by the complainant. In human rights cases, the loss which is claimed is not based on the basis that the loss was foreseeable. This is not the test.

2. The Importance of Making a Claim for Reinstatement

You should always make a reinstatement claim. You may be thinking that there is no way that you wish to return to this place of employment, but believe me when I say the company does not want you coming back even more.

There are strategic reasons to make a reinstatement claim. The claim can be used to negotiate a more effective remedy. Also, a claim for a prospective loss of income to the date of the hearing, which can be supported by the reinstatement request, is not taxable income, an important issue when debating settlement. A sum paid to give up the claim for reinstatement is also likely not taxable income.

It would be expected that, apart from the need to seek other employment (i.e., mitigation issues), or otherwise an application of "principled discretion" (e.g., the closing of the employer's business or intervening unrelated medical issues), an order of reinstatement would be accompanied by an award for lost income to the date of reinstatement.

Reinstatement is obviously a very powerful remedy. Apart from the order itself, the request for the order will more readily support a lost income claim to the date of hearing and also may be used to buttress a plea for a prospective income loss beyond the date of hearing when the reinstatement order has been denied.

Instatement means that the employer is ordered to provide the employee a position of employment, which is different from the last position held.

You can use the cases in this chapter to support an argument for a lost income claim to the date of the hearing. This was the decision made by the Human Rights Tribunal in *Fair v. Hamilton-Wentworth District School*

Board[7] in which an order for lost income was determined for the eight-and-a-half-year period between the dismissal and the date of reinstatement in the sum of approximately $420,000.

The same result followed in *Ontario Human Rights Commission and Karumanchiri et al v. Liquor Control Board of Ontario* 8 CHRR D/4076 (Baum) in which the complainant Karumanchiri was instated to the promoted position of Chief Chemist, an order which was accompanied by a sum awarded for the wage differential from April 1, 1979, to the date of the order in March 1987. This decision was affirmed on review by the Divisional Court 9 CHRR D/4868, although the award for lost income differential was not a subject raised by the employer on the judicial review.

This was also the conclusion of the Board of Inquiry in *McKinnon v. Correctional Services #3* in which the Board ordered that the complainant and his spouse each be instated to the rank of OM16 and receive appropriate salary arrears from the date of the initially unsuccessful application for such employment from March 1989 to the date of the award in April 1998, nine years later.

2.1 Future lost income when reinstatement is not allowed

You can also argue for a future lost income claim where reinstatement is not allowed or where you are medically unable to return to work, provided that the medical inability to work has been caused by the company's wrongdoing, which is a human rights violation.

The issue of whether a Tribunal can and should award a prospective income loss was considered, but not decided in the 2010 decision of *McLean v. DY 4 Systems*,[8] a case which was based on a perceived disability. The applicant sought lost income to the date of the intended retirement on her 65th birthday, which was eleven months beyond the date of the hearing. To complicate matters slightly, there was no claim for reinstatement advanced, which became the argument of the employer. It was not contested that the Tribunal had the power to make such an order for future loss of income.

The employer had submitted that a contingency discount should be applied to reflect the likelihood of risk. The Tribunal did not decide the issue as written submissions were requested. No further decision followed. The Tribunal did make this statement on the issue of prospective loss:

> *In my view, the Tribunal must have regard to the circumstances of the specific party, as discernable from the evidence before it, in making any compensatory award. In employment cases, the question of whether the party has asked for reinstatement is relevant, but, in the absence of a specific provision in the Code, I do not think it can be determinative. The Tribunal must take into account all*

7   *Fair v. Hamilton-Wentworth District School Board*, 2013, accessed September 2014.
    http://www.canlii.org/en/on/onhrt/doc/2013/2013hrto440/2013hrto440.html
8   *McLean v. DY 4 Systems*, 2010, accessed September 2014.
    http://www.canlii.org/en/on/onhrt/doc/2010/2010hrto1107/2010hrto1107.html

of the facts established by the evidence. Here, there are circumstances that in my view might warrant a prospective wages and benefits award, or an order even in the absence of a request for reinstatement.

[93] *The respondent admits that, but for the incidents at issue in this Application, they had no performance concerns that would have warranted terminating the applicant's employment. The applicant enjoyed her work and had no plans to leave.*

[94] *There is no question in this case of any request for an indeterminate prospective award; in fact, the contemplated period is fairly brief. The applicant has admitted that she would have retired when she turned 65.*

[95] *The applicant was 62 years old when her employment was terminated. She has a high school education; it appears that her skills were developed entirely on the job — she has no "paper qualifications." She has significant disabilities. It is foreseeable that a person in these circumstances might have great difficulty finding alternative employment. The applicant's experience in her attempts to mitigate have borne this out. I conclude that she is not likely to find permanent employment prior to her 65th birthday.*

[96] *If the applicant finds employment on a short-term or permanent basis, corresponding deductions can be made in the relevant 15-month timeframe between the date of the hearing and the date the applicant would have retired in any event (between January 20, 2010 and April 26, 2011).*

[97] *The respondent suggested that I apply a "contingency factor" of 20%, citing Morris v. British Columbia Railway Co. (2003), 46 C.H.R.R. D/162, 2003 BCHRT 14. However, in that case, there was at least some evidence of "on-going corporate restructuring and down-sizing." By contrast, all the evidence here was that the respondent was in the fortunate position of doing extremely well and hiring more staff. Further, in this case the respondent had no concerns with the applicant's performance on the job; while she may not have received as much in bonus payments, she may have received some such payments or a raise in pay, which possibility will not be reflected in this order.*

[98] *There remains the issue of whether an Order that would compensate the applicant from the last day of hearing until the applicant turns 65 on April 26, 2011, is appropriate. The issue of whether I have the jurisdiction to order reinstatement where it has not specifically been requested has not been addressed at all. Nor have I had full representations from counsel in respect of an order that would require the respondent to pay the applicant on an ongoing basis from the last day of hearing until April 26, 2011, with a reporting arrangement that would allow for deduction for any*

income earned from alternative employment engaged in by the applicant during this period.

[99] I will remain seized of this narrow issue so that counsel may have the opportunity to make full representations.

Reference was made to the decision of *McKee v. Hayes-Dana Inc.* (1992), 17 C.H.R.R. D/79, an age discrimination case in which an award was made to compensate the complainant from age 57 to 65, some of which was prospective, that is beyond the date of the hearing. McKee was terminated on August 16, 1985, at age 57. He had been employed with Hayes-Dana for 32 years. An award was made for lost wages from October 1, 1985, to McKee's 65th birthday through to 1993. The decision awarding McKee lost income to this date was released on April 22, 1992, and there was a prospective component of at least eight months. McKee's precise date of birth does not appear in the decision.

The decision of the Tribunal in *Pilon v. Cornwall (City)*[9] followed in January 2012 in which the applicant sought a claim for lost income to age 55 beyond the date of the hearing. On this issue, the Tribunal stated that such an order would be made only in an unusual context:

> *As noted by the respondent, the Tribunal has not yet made an order of post-hearing wage loss. In my view such an award would be extraordinary and not likely to be made except in exceptional circumstances. One reason for this conclusion flows from my view that the obligation of the applicant to mitigate his or her damages runs together with a claim to damages for lost wages. It is obviously impossible to assess an applicant's ongoing efforts to mitigate a wage loss post hearing. As such, any award of post-hearing damages for lost wages would be almost entirely speculative in the majority of cases.*

It is true that the assessment of a future loss is not mathematical. This should not deny the application of the concept. It would be prudent to advance a claim for reinstatement to support a claim for a prospective income loss.

The Canadian Human Rights Tribunal in *McAvinn v. Strait Bridge Crossing Ltd.*[10] made an order requiring that the first available position of a bridge patroller be awarded to the complainant in its decision of November 2001. The commencement date of the lost income award was May 31, 1997. The award stated that failing such an offer of alternate employment, the total lost income was to be set at a ten-year period. The contingent prospective loss was set for a time period of six years and seven months.

An award of $512,000 for a future lost income award was made in the sexual harassment case of *The City of Calgary v. Canadian Union of Public Employees*,[11] given the medical evidence that the victim could never

9 *Pilon v. Cornwall (City)*, 2012, accessed September 2014.
    http://www.canlii.org/en/on/onhrt/doc/2012/2012hrto177/2012hrto177.html
10 *McAvinn v. Strait Bridge Crossing Ltd.*, 2001, accessed September 2014.
    http://www.canlii.org/en/ca/chrt/doc/2001/2001canlii7954/2001canlii7954.html
11 *The City of Calgary v. Canadian Union of Public Employees*, 2013, accessed September 2014.
    http://www.canlii.org/en/ab/abgaa/doc/2013/2013canlii88297/2013canlii88297.html

return to work. The award was reduced by 10 percent to reflect the possibility of part-time employment and by a further 2.5 percent to account for an immediate payment.

2.2 Lost Opportunity

In a fact situation where you assert that you were denied an offer of employment, the case is more difficult. Apart from the usual argument that the decision was in some way influenced by a human rights violation, you must show that, absent such a violation, you would likely have been hired. For example, if it can be shown that the decision was somehow influenced by race, the employer may argue that there was still no possibility that you would have been hired, in any event, in that the requisite skills or experience were lacking.

The Tribunal will conduct a review to determine if there was a reasonable possibility that you would have been hired, presuming no human rights violation, and if so, it will then proceed to assess the degree of such probability. An example of such a case is the 2007 decision in *Seguin v. Great Blue Heron Charity Casino*[12] in which the Tribunal concluded that there was a 50 percent chance that the applicant, who was denied the opportunity to be hired for cleaning services due to gender, would have otherwise been hired for this position. The test used was "reasonable possibility." The Divisional Court set aside the remedy decision, not on its merits, but rather on a technical argument.[13]

A similar analysis was completed in the April 2013 decision of *Rocha v. Pardons and Waivers of Canada*.[14] The issue in this case was whether the applicant would have been confirmed in permanent employment following an unpaid training period. The final position contained a bookkeeping component with which the applicant was unfamiliar. The same award of 50 percent followed for the period of unemployment which was 11 weeks.

3. Provincial and Territorial Reinstatement Remedies

Reinstatement is a common concept in Canadian jurisdictions. The legislation varies but typically provides authority to the human rights tribunal to take such action to remedy the wrong doing or alternatively specifically empowers reinstatement.

It is not a default remedy as may be expected in arbitral jurisprudence. The comparison is offered to put the Ontario remedy in some degree of perspective. In the remaining jurisdictions, reinstatement is viewed as a discretionary remedy and has been ordered when considered appropriate with due regard to all factors in play.

---

12 *Seguin v. Great Blue Heron Charity Casino*, 2007, accessed September 2014.
http://www.canlii.org/en/on/onhrt/doc/2007/2007hrto33/2007hrto33.html
13 *Great Blue Heron Charity Casino v. Ontario Human Rights Commission*, 2008, accessed September 2014.
http://www.canlii.org/en/on/onscdc/doc/2008/2008canlii45003/2008canlii45003.html
14 *Rocha v. Pardons and Waivers of Canada*, 2013, accessed September 2014.
http://www.canlii.org/en/on/onhrt/doc/2013/2013hrto537/2013hrto537.html

3.1 The Federal Act

You will have a much better chance of obtaining a back-to-work order under the *Canadian Human Rights Act*. Reinstatement has been awarded comparatively frequently under the terms of the *Canadian Human Rights Act* which by section 53 provides specifically for such a remedy:

> *53 (2) If at the conclusion of the inquiry the member or panel finds that the complaint is substantiated, the member or panel may, subject to section 54, make an order against the person found to be engaging or to have engaged in the discriminatory practice and include in the order any of the following terms that the member or panel considers appropriate:*
>
> *(b) that the person make available to the victim of the discriminatory practice, on the first reasonable occasion, the rights, opportunities or privileges that are being or were denied the victim as a result of the practice;*

The Federal Tribunal appears more prone to the order as revealed in the decision of *Pitawanakwat v. Department of the Secretary of State*[15] in which the Tribunal found that reinstatement was unworkable, at least in the position sought, a conclusion which did not deny the complainant from reinstatement yet to an alternate position.

It was the employee who sought judicial review of this decision by which, amongst other issues, she sought reinstatement to her last position held. The Federal Court agreed with this submission and allowed this remedy.[16] In so doing it looked to the following passage from Chief Justice Dickson for guidance as to remedy:

> *In Canadian National Railway Co. v. Canada (Canadian Human Rights Commission? 1987 CanLII 109 (SCC), [1987] 1 S.C.R. 1114. Chief Justice Dickson stated, at page 1134:*
>
> *Human rights legislation is intended to give rise, amongst other things, to individual rights of vital importance, rights capable of enforcement, in the final analysis, in a court of law. I recognize that in the construction of such legislation the words of the Act must be given their plain meaning, but it is equally important that the rights enunciated be given their full recognition and effect. <u>We should not search for ways and means to minimize those rights and to enfeeble their proper impact.</u> [Underlining added for emphasis comes from the original Federal Court decision.]*

The Court in this instance determined that the remedy provided by the Tribunal weakened the relief provided by the Act:

> *The explanation of the Tribunal for limiting its order of reinstatement of the principal applicant to offices of the Department outside*

---

15 *Pitawanakwat v. Department of the Secretary of State*, 1992, accessed September 2014.
   http://www.canlii.org/en/ca/chrt/doc/1992/1992canlii936/1992canlii936.html
16 *Pitawanakwat v. Canada (Attorney General)*, 1994, accessed September 2014.
   http://www.canlii.org/en/ca/fct/doc/1994/1994canlii3485/1994canlii3485.html

of Saskatchewan was, I conclude, a ways or means, however well intended, of enfeebling the proper impact of rights conferred by the Canadian Human Rights Act on those, such as the principal applicant, who have been discriminated against by removal from employment on a prohibited ground of discrimination.

The Federal Court determined that the applicant could not be responsible for the issues which may have resulted from her reinstatement as it was she who was the innocent party:

The "recipe for disaster" envisaged by the Tribunal is an issue to be dealt with by the Department that refused to continue to employ her on a prohibited ground of discrimination. It is not a justification for failing to grant to the principal applicant the full remedy of reinstatement, where it is acknowledged by the Tribunal that reinstatement is appropriate.

The order of the Tribunal was set aside and the complainant was restored to her last position.

A further example of such an award is the 2001 decision of the Canadian Human Rights Tribunal in *Nkwazi v. Canada (Correctional Service),*[17] which spoke of the "duty" of the tribunal to attempt to restore the complainant to "the position she would have been in, but for," in a complaint based on race and colour:

As noted above, where a complaint of discrimination is found to be substantiated, it is the duty of a human rights tribunal to attempt to restore the complainant to the position that she would have been in, but for the discrimination. In this case, Ms. Neufeld testified that the RPC always needed casual employees, and that the renewal of a casual employee's contract was almost automatic, unless there were performance concerns. This testimony is borne out by Ms. Nkwazi's own experience with nine contract renewals, as well as by the experience of other RPC employees. I am satisfied that, had Ms. Neufeld not acted in a discriminatory fashion towards Ms. Nkwazi, Ms. Nkwazi would still be employed at the RPC. As a result, I order CSC to reinstate Ms. Nkwazi to a position of casual nurse at the RPC at the first reasonable opportunity.

The reference to the "duty" was repeated but phrased somewhat differently, as a duty to restore her to the position that she would have been in, which in this instance was reinstatement, as opposed to a duty to reinstate, in the 2006 decision of *Desormeaux v. Ottawa-Carleton Regional Transit.*[18] The complaint was based on adverse treatment due to a medical disability. This decision was set aside on a preliminary review and subsequently restored by the Court of Appeal.[19] These latter decisions did not deal with the issue of remedy. The Tribunal stated:

---

17 *Nkwazi v. Canada (Correctional Service)*, 2001, accessed September 2014.
  http://www.canlii.org/en/ca/chrt/doc/2001/2001canlii6296/2001canlii6296.html
18 *Desormeaux v. Ottawa-Carleton Regional Transit*, 2003, accessed September 2014.
  http://www.canlii.org/en/ca/chrt/doc/2003/2003chrt2/2003chrt2.html
19 *Desormeaux v. Ottawa (City)*, 2005, accessed September 2014.
  http://www.canlii.org/en/ca/fca/doc/2005/2005fca311/2005fca311.html

A. Reinstatement

[115] Where a complaint of discrimination is found to be substantiated, it is the duty of a human rights tribunal to attempt to restore the complainant to the position that she would have been in, but for the discrimination. In this case, that duty is best discharged by reinstating Ms. Desormeaux to her position as a bus operator with OC Transpo. Ms. Desormeaux should receive the seniority and benefits, including pension benefits, that she would have had, had she been continuously employed by OC Transpo. She should, as well, receive any training necessary to update her skills and re-familiarize her with workplace policies and procedures.

[116] In reinstating Ms. Desormeaux to the position of bus operator, I leave it to OC Transpo, in consultation with Ms. Desormeaux and her union, to identify a position for Ms. Desormeaux which will minimize the impact that Ms. Desormeaux's intermittent absences will have on service delivery. I further direct OC Transpo to consult with Ms. Desormeaux and her union, as well as with Dr. Meehan, if necessary, in order to determine what steps can safely be taken in order to minimize Ms. Desormeaux's absences from work, without her having to resort to driving while under the influence of medication. In this regard, I note that the Amalgamated Transit Union has undertaken to fully co-operate in the implementation of any order that the Tribunal may make against OC Transpo with respect to Ms. Desormeaux's return to the workplace.

A similar order was made by the federal Tribunal in the 1999 decision of *Bernard v. Waycobah Board of Education*,[20] ordering not only reinstatement to the first available position, but also lost income until the effective date of such event. The complaint was based on a perceived mental disability.

With respect to reinstatement, I order that Waycobah Band Council provide to Ms. Bernard, at the first reasonable opportunity, a position as secretary similar in scope and responsibility to the one that she held as school secretary. Until commencement of such employment, Waycobah Band Council shall continue to pay to Ms. Bernard, from the date of this decision, a salary of $325.00 per week.

In the event that a reasonable offer of employment is not forthcoming within a reasonable period of time, or should any dispute arise concerning the terms of such an offer, I hereby retain jurisdiction to hear more evidence and to deal with the matter upon request of any or all of the parties.

A further award of reinstatement was found in *Uzoaba v. Canada (Correctional Service)*[21] in which the decision was made 13 years following

20 *Bernard v. Waycobah Board of Education*, 1999, accessed September 2014.
   http://www.canlii.org/en/ca/chrt/doc/1999/1999canlii1914/1999canlii1914.html
21 *Uzoaba v. Canada (Correctional Service)*, 1994, accessed September 2014.
   http://www.canlii.org/en/ca/chrt/doc/1994/1994canlii1636/1994canlii1636.html

the filing of the complaint and in circumstances where the complainant held considerable animosity to the employer:

> *The Tribunal has given careful consideration to the issue of reinstatement. Given that the Complainant has been out of the workforce for over 13 years, and also having regard to the evident anger and resentment that the Complainant feels towards his employer, the Tribunal has concerns about returning Dr. Uzoaba to the workforce. On the other hand, the Tribunal is cognizant of the devastating effect that these events have had upon the Complainant and his family. Having given the issue careful consideration, and keeping in mind the remedial nature of the legislation, the Tribunal has concluded that the only way that Dr. Uzoaba can be adequately compensated is to direct that he be reinstated into a position within CSC.*

The complainant was reinstated not to the position held by him when the action arose, but rather to a higher position which he successfully asserted he would have attained, absent adverse conduct by the employer. The employer had argued that the *Public Service Act* mandated promotions be based on merit, a position which was argued again unsuccessfully in the Federal Court on judicial review.[22]

Reinstatement is not considered an unusual remedy under the federal Act. Many decisions have routinely ordered this relief as the means by which the complainant has been restored to the former position.

3.2 Ontario

Most human rights codes specifically empower the tribunal to order reinstatement as a remedy. Ontario's Code does not specifically give this authority. There is nothing in the wording of the legislation which suggests that such a remedy should be limited to exclude or otherwise limit the granting of a reinstatement order. The Code clearly allows for a remedy as a restitution for "other than through monetary compensation":

> *45.2 (1) On an application under section 34, the Tribunal may make one or more of the following orders if the Tribunal determines that a party to the application has infringed a right under Part I of another party to the application:*
>
> 1. *An order directing the party who infringed the right to pay monetary compensation to the party whose right was infringed for loss arising out of the infringement, including compensation for injury to dignity, feelings and self-respect.*
>
> 2. *An order directing the party who infringed the right to* **make restitution to the party whose right was infringed, other than through monetary compensation,** *for loss arising out of the infringement, including restitution for injury to dignity, feelings and self-respect.*

---

22 *Canada (Attorney General) v. Uzoaba*, 1995, accessed September 2014.
  http://www.canlii.org/en/ca/fct/doc/1995/1995canlii3589/1995canlii3589.html

3. *An order directing any party to the application to do anything that, in the opinion of the Tribunal, the party ought to do to promote compliance with this Act. 2006, c. 30, s. 5.*

The analysis which follows will show that reinstatement was considered "the prime remedy" for many years in Ontario. In recent years, the frequency of such orders has, for unknown reasons, become less evident.

You should reference the following cases when arguing for a reinstatement remedy. All in all, reinstatement will be a discretionary order, which means it is certainly not a lock and even if you win the case, it does not necessarily mean that there will be a reinstatement order made.

The recent decision of *Fair v. Hamilton-Wentworth District School Board*,[23] which allowed for such a remedy, no doubt headed to higher authority, may prove to be the bellwether.

Early Ontario cases from 1975 to 1999 showed a strong bias in favour of reinstatement. These decisions speak of reinstatement as basically a default remedy. These older cases are summarized here because they have been ignored in modern decisions, which should not happen. If you are arguing a reinstatement case, chances are that the employer lawyer and the Tribunal will never have read them before.

Note that these cases are not available online so you will need to find them in the law library published by CHRR or some libraries such as Osgoode Hall Law School which have the full text of early Ontario Board of Inquiry decisions available.

The decision of *Segrave v. Zeller's Limited* (Lederman) was made in September of 1975 and is reflective of the strong inclination at the time to order reinstatement as a remedy. The male complainant had applied for the advertised position of personnel management trainee in response to which he was advised that only women were considered for this position. He then inquired about a further vacant position of credit management trainee. He was not considered for this position as he was in violation of the company rule which prevented consideration of any candidate who had been separated or divorced within the immediately preceding two years.

A successful complaint was brought based on sex and marital status. The company was ordered to retain an independent agency, in consultation with the Human Rights Commission, to conduct an interview of the complainant and to use the company's tests and qualifications, amended to be in conformity with the Code, to determine if the complainant could qualify for either the personnel management or the credit management trainee positions.

The complainant maintained an independent divorce-consulting business which took an average of 12 hours per week. The independent agency was ordered to determine if the company had any policy which would not allow such an external business provided that it was "a genuine policy and not

---

23 *Fair v. Hamilton-Wentworth District School Board*, 2013, accessed September 2014.
    http://www.canlii.org/en/on/onhrt/doc/2013/2013hrto440/2013hrto440.html

recently manufactured solely to exclude the complainant." Provided that the complainant passed the testing, the employer was ordered to offer to him a position of employment.

The first decision made by a Board of Inquiry (Cumming) under the 1981 Human Rights Code was that of *Cameron v. Nel-Gor Castle Nursing Home*, 1984 5 CHRR D/2170. The complaint was brought by a person suffering from a medical handicap defined as "congenital syndactyly," which was described as "a defective left upper extremity." She had undergone several surgeries on her left hand which resulted in the middle, ring, and little finger being shorter than normal. She had sought and was declined employment as a nursing aide with the respondent nursing home.

Having found a breach of the Code, the Board then considered remedy and noted that the complainant had not requested an order that an offer of employment be extended to her, having as the Board noted, secured employment elsewhere. The Board, nonetheless, made such an order, concluding that this relief should be "the primary remedy to a Complainant who has been denied her right to equal treatment with respect to employment because of handicap." It is evident that this order was made to give punch to the Code to demonstrate reinstatement as such a default remedy.

The Board of Inquiry in its November 1984 decision of *Mark v. Porcupine General Hospital* (Cumming) 6 CHRRD/2538 found liability against the employer due to its decision to terminate the complainant due to marital status. Although the remedy provided was not reinstatement due to particularities of the legislation as it then stood, the Board ordered that the employer provide to the complainant notices of any vacancies from the date of the award in November of 1984 through to the end of 1986 and to consider her application on its merits and in compliance with the Code. As to the principled position on remedy, the Board stated that the prime relief should be reinstatement:

> *The practical solution in the instant situation would have been for the hospital to offer Mrs. Mark a position in another department, if and when a suitable one became available. The evidence is uncertain as to whether another suitable position has been open at any time since her employment was terminated, and it is unknown as to who, Mrs. Mark or the Hospital, failed to take any initiative in this regard. Perhaps there were negotiations in contemplated settlement of the complaint; it would be improper, of course, for this Board to hear of any such negotiations which must be on a without prejudice basis. I only raise the above to indicate the most appropriate remedy in the instant situation, and the one clearly suitable in a situation where, in a layperson's sense of the word, both parties might well be considered "innocent." As I emphasized in Cameron (supra, at D/2196) para 18523) the prime remedy in an "employment case" where a complainant has been denied her rights to equality of treatment, is an order under paragraph 40(1) (a) directing that an offer of employment be made. The remedy*

provisions should be construed liberally to achieve the purposes and policies of the legislation: Rand, supra at D/956. An overriding objective of the remedies is to achieve restitution:

> *that is, the eradication of the harmful effects of a respondent's actions on the complainant, and the placing of a complainant in the same position in which she would have been, had her human rights not been infringed by the respondent. (Cameron, supra at D/2196, para 18523)*

Reinstatement was not ordered in this instance due to the particular context of this case under the legislation in existence at that time:

> *The practical solution is for Mrs. Mark to be given the opportunity of employment in another department. However, given first, that she is no longer an employee of the Hospital, and second, that the freedom in hiring extended to an employer under paragraph 23(d) allows the employer to not hire her in a department where her husband is also employed. I do not think an order should direct that she necessarily be offered an employment position in the maintenance and housekeeping department.*

The Board of Inquiry in *Barnard v. Canadian Corps of Commissionaires* (Friedland), a decision made in January of 1985 considered the complaint made by Mr. Barnard that he had been denied his application for membership with the respondent based on nationality. The complainant had served in the Indian Army during the Second World War. He had ceased to be a British subject when India obtained its independence. The purpose of the Corps was to assist veterans to obtain employment in the civilian community.

Liability was found. The remedy granted was an order that the Corps "consider as soon as reasonably possible any renewal of his application for membership." The decision was appealed to Divisional Court but no issue was raised as to remedy in this forum. The liability decision was upheld.

The decision of the Board of Inquiry in the March 1987 decision in *Ontario Human Rights Commission and Karumanchiri et al v. Liquor Control Board of Ontario* 8 CHRR D/4076 (Baum) also found in favour of Karumanchiri and ordered that he be instated to a higher level position. This decision was affirmed on a judicial review application in the Divisional Court 9 CHRR D/4868.

On review, the employer raised the issue of the jurisdiction of the Board to instate the complainant into the promoted position. Rosenberg J., writing for the unanimous panel, stated that the wording of the Code which allowed the Board to "direct the party to do anything" were to be read liberally and broadly and upheld the decision of Baum.

Instatement was also considered and awarded in *Wiens v. Inco Metals* (Cumming) 9 CHRR D/4975, a decision made in February of 1988. The applicant had been employed with Inco Metals since June of 1974 as a labourer. The company used a process for the recovery of pure nickel from source materials known as the Inco Pressure Carbonyl (IPC) process. The company refused to employ women of child-bearing age in the IPC area due to its fear that the exposure to nickel carbonyl gas may cause harm to a fetus. A finding of adverse treatment was made.

The remedy ordered was that the company provide appropriate training and following the successful completion of same, the first available position in the IPC, which was to exclude consideration of seniority and "notwithstanding any provision in any collective bargaining agreement."

An order of reinstatement was also made in the August 1989 decision of the Board of Inquiry (Hubbard) in *Morgoch v. City of Ottawa*. The complainant applied for a position of a firefighter, which application was denied as Morgoch suffered from seasonal allergies. Liability was found based on adverse treatment due to a handicap. On the issue of remedy, as the application had been not been processed due to the initial disclosure of the medical issue, it was ordered that the applicant be required to demonstrate the success in the fitness and agility testing requirements, and following same, that he be offered employment on terms as agreed between the parties, or as may be later ordered by the Board.

The Ontario Court of Appeal in *Naraine v. Ford* reversed the award made by the Board of reinstatement. The initial order granted by the Board of Inquiry (Constance Backhouse) in December of 1996, in *Naraine v. Ford Motor Co. of Canada #5* 28 CHRR D/267, is nonetheless instructive of the issues to be considered by the decision maker in such a circumstance. The Board noted that arbitral jurisprudence had determined that "so long as the employment relationship appears to be viable, reinstatement orders will issue" and further observed that the remedial powers found in the Code were similar to those given to labour arbitrators. The Board stated:

> *Adjudicators under the Code obviously have the authority to issue orders of reinstatement, and can have resort to the principles and values articulated in arbitration awards insofar as these conform to the goals and purposes of human rights legislation.*

The Board also noted that in the arbitral case law, reinstatement orders are the norm even where the parties may have exhibited a long history of interpersonal tension and confrontation. In ordering reinstatement, the Board saw this remedy as the means by which the remedy of restitution may be attained:

> *After reflecting on the problems inherent in quantifying the value of reinstatement, and considering all of the other factors present in this case, I have concluded that only the remedy of reinstatement would properly serve as restitution to Mr. Naraine. Reinstatement is the remedy which most fully attempts to put Mr. Naraine back into the position he would have enjoyed had the wrong not occurred, to "make whole" his loss resulting from the violation of the Code. Reinstatement can also serve the educational purposes of*

human rights legislation in that it will signify to all Ford supervisors, employees, and members of the wider community, through a concrete and highly visible order, that discriminatory conduct will be redressed by the board of inquiry.

The Board also made an order that the reinstatement process would be one which would be subject to guidelines issued by the Board to minimize conflict in this process:

It is important for both parties, and critical to the public interest, that steps be taken to enhance the likelihood of Mr. Naraine's successful reintegration to the Ford work force. The purposes of the Code will only be realized to the extent that the parties are able to resolve their past differences and move towards a working environment which values racial integration and equality. Boards of Inquiry have jurisdiction to ask the parties to try to work out the details of reintegration between themselves, while remaining seized of the matter in a supervisory capacity should there be unforeseen complications in complying with the order; see, for example, Canada (Attorney-General) v. Grover (1994) 24 CHRR D/390 (F.C.T.D.). It is also open to a board of inquiry to issue guidelines to accompany an order of reinstatement that will assist the parties in effecting a successful reconciliation. This appears to be precisely the sort of case which would benefit from this flexibility of approach. The evidence in this case suggests that an order for reinstatement may not result in a seamless re-entry into the automotive plant for Mr. Naraine. To attempt to maximize the prospects for success, movement is required from both sides to this dispute.

The above analyses were not the subject of adverse commentary by the Court of Appeal which set aside the order of reinstatement for other reasons as noted above.

The Board of Inquiry in *McKinnon v. Ministry of Correctional Services #3* (Hubbard) in April of 1998 found adverse treatment due to race. The complainant was ordered to be promoted to the rank of OM16. The evidence had shown that all OM14 level positions, such being the one to which the complainant had applied unsuccessfully in March of 1989, had been re-graded to OM16.

The Board also ordered that the complainant's spouse, who was an employee of the same Ministry, although not a party complainant, also be instated into such a position. The apparent logic behind such an order was that it was intended to redress the harm done to the complainant for adverse treatment afforded to him, which included wrongs done to his spouse as a means of reprisal to the complainant.

Modern human rights decisions are bereft of any acknowledgement of the jurisprudence set out above. The cited decisions have not been referenced, either in support of, opposed to, accepted, rejected, or distinguished, in the recent analyses pondering the award of reinstatement.

The words of then-Professor Cummings which described as the order of reinstatement as the "prime remedy" have somehow, for unknown reasons, fallen to the wayside. That which was first set out so fundamentally as the default remedy, admittedly strong words, has been recently characterized as "rarely requested or ordered," words which, it is submitted, are not fairly descriptive of the remedy, even in a modern context.

The following discuss more recent cases that can be referenced in your own case.

The decision of the Ontario Human Rights Tribunal in *Dhamrait v. JVI Canada*[24] in May of 2010 awarded reinstatement. The company was an assembly and packaging business with nine employees. The goal of shaping the remedy, the Tribunal noted, is to restore that which should have been, which is an application of the make whole remedy. On the facts of this case, the employer was facing the need to reduce its staffing requirements. On this issue, the Tribunal found this decision would not have adversely affected the complainant.

The June 2010 decision of the Ontario Human Rights Tribunal followed in *Krieger v. Toronto Police Services Board*[25] in which reinstatement was again awarded. The Tribunal did observe that awards of reinstatement historically were "rarely requested or ordered." In this case the Tribunal spoke to this issue:

> *[182] While reinstatement orders are rarely requested or ordered in human rights cases, they are "normally" ordered in arbitral cases where a violation of a griever's rights has been found, unless there are "concerns that the employment relationship is no longer viable" Alberta Union of Public Employees v. Lethbridge Community College, 2004 SCC 28 (CanLII), [2004] S.C.R. 727, 2004 SCC 28 (CanLII), at para. 56. The goal of human rights legislation, which is remedial in nature, is to put the applicant in the position that he or she would have been in had the discrimination not taken place. See Impact Interiors Inc. v. Ontario (Human Rights Commission) (1998), 35 C.H.R.R. D/477 (Ont. C.A.). Where viable, reinstatement is sometimes the only remedy that can give effect to this principle.*

The Tribunal pointed to the size of the business as a large and sophisticated employer, an issue also noted in the discussion of reinstatement as the appropriate remedy in the subsequent decision below. The short employment history was not considered a factor in the reinstatement remedy:

> *It would be inappropriate to use the applicant's relatively short service record as a factor weighing against reinstatement in a human rights case. The factors taken into account by an arbitrator in deciding remedies for a termination grievance may not be*

24 *Dhamrait v. JVI Canada*, 2010, accessed September 2014.
   http://www.canlii.org/en/on/onhrt/doc/2010/2010hrto1085/2010hrto1085.html
25 *Krieger v. Toronto Police Services Board*, 2010, accessed September 2014.
   http://www.canlii.org/en/on/onhrt/doc/2010/2010hrto1361/2010hrto1361.html

congruent with the considerations applicable to determining remedies under the Code.

An instatement order was made by the Tribunal in *Tearne v. Windsor (City)*[26] in an age discrimination case. The applicant had been offered employment as a part-time arena attendant to supplement his retirement income. Liability was found due to the failure of the employer to show a bona fide occupational requirement in the medical testing it had requested. The order made by the Tribunal was the applicant provide an updated medical certificate from his physician, as he had done initially, after which the City was allowed to perform such Code-compliant medical testing as required and following the successful completion of same, that he be offered the employment in question.

The Human Rights Tribunal in *Macan v. Strongco*[27] spoke to this issue in May 2013. The Tribunal in this case noted that there was jurisdiction under the Code to reinstate, yet repeated the theme that "this order is rarely requested or ordered in human rights cases." The Tribunal continued to state that where reinstatement had been ordered, the applicant had been a unionized employee for a large employer as in *Krieger* above. It was also suggested in this instance that a factor in awarding reinstatement in *Dhamrait* was that the applicant held an unskilled position, a sentiment which was not expressed by the decision maker in *Dhamrait* itself. The Tribunal in this case was obviously against the idea of reinstatement.

If you are arguing for reinstatement, you can count on the employer counsel to use this case against you. The purpose of showing the early history of the reinstatement remedy under the Code is to shake off this notion that reinstatement is "rarely requested or ordered," as this just isn't so.

Notwithstanding all of the above, the decision of *Fair v. Hamilton-Wentworth District School Board* (see footnote 7) released on March 14, 2013, ordered reinstatement. The Tribunal had found that the employer had treated the applicant unfairly due to a disability by failing to accommodate her disability-related needs from April 2003 and then by terminating her employment on July 9, 2004. The Tribunal noted that the remedial objective of human rights legislation is to make the applicant "whole." It also found that had the employer been properly accommodating the applicant, she would have been returned to full-time employment in June of 2003, in one of the two positions which were then available.

It was also noted that there was no personal animosity between the parties and that the employer was a large entity with a sophisticated management structure. All factors considered, there was no prejudice caused by the reinstatement request. The argument advanced by the employer that reinstatement would be unfair due to the passing of eight and a half years from termination to the date of the remedy was not successful. The delay was determined not to be to any failing of the applicant.

---

26 *Tribunal in Tearne v. Windsor (City)*, 2011, accessed September 2014.
   http://www.canlii.org/en/on/onhrt/doc/2011/2011hrto2294/2011hrto2294.html
27 *Macan v. Strongco*, 2013, accessed September 2014.
   http://www.canlii.org/en/on/onhrt/doc/2013/2013hrto841/2013hrto841.html

No matter what the origin, clearly the tribunal is empowered to consider reinstatement as an exercise of its discretionary remedial authority. This case will be watched closely as it is reviewed on the inevitable judicial review application.

3.3 British Columbia

The BC statute has a provision which is similar to that of the federal act. It states that the Tribunal may:

> *(i) make available to the person discriminated against the right, opportunity or privilege that, in the opinion of the member or panel, the person was denied contrary to this Code;*

The interpretation of this provision allows the Tribunal to consider in its discretion whether reinstatement is viable in the context of the facts before it. It is not clear on whom the onus to prove a proper circumstance for such a remedy may lie, but given that it is never considered a presumptive remedy, it is a fair bet that it rests on the party seeking the order.

A good example of a review of the contextual issues to determine the propriety of such a remedy is seen in the recent 2008 decision of *Kalyn v. Vancouver Island Health Authority (VIHA)*:[28]

> *The essence of both Mr. MacDonald's and Mr. McKenzie's opposition to Ms. Kalyn's reinstatement is focused on their view of her complaints against VIHA and the impact on them. I have rejected Mr. MacDonald's testimony that Ms. Kalyn was confrontational and negative. VIHA has not proven that Ms. Kalyn's co-workers do not trust her. Of the witnesses who would be directly affected by Ms. Kalyn's reinstatement, Mr. McKenzie expressed the greatest reservations. Mr. Cabrita, on the other hand, saw reinstatement as viable. I give little weight to Mr. McKenzie's evidence in this regard as he was, in my view, implicated in VIHA's discriminatory conduct toward Ms. Kalyn and his opinion is likely affected by self-interest.*

> *[540] VIHA's arguments and evidence in opposition to reinstatement were largely the same as its arguments and evidence in support of its reasons to terminate Ms. Kalyn's employment. My assessment of that evidence is discussed above and I do not repeat it here. It is sufficient to say that I did not accept those reasons and found that the termination of Ms. Kalyn's employment was a result of sex discrimination. In light of all of the evidence, I am persuaded that reinstatement is an appropriate remedy to the discrimination Ms. Kalyn has suffered.*

A similar issue was reviewed in *J.J. v. School District No. 43*[29] in which a finding was made of adverse treatment due to gender. Reinstatement was considered but not ordered due to the finding that it was not a proper

---

28 *Kalyn v. Vancouver Island Health Authority (No.3)*, 2008, accessed September 2014.
   http://www.canlii.org/en/bc/bchrt/doc/2008/2008bchrt377/2008bchrt377.html#par529
29 *J.J. v. School District No. 43 (No.5)*, 2008, accessed September 2014.
   http://www.canlii.org/en/bc/bchrt/doc/2008/2008bchrt360/2008bchrt360.html#par505

remedy in the circumstances based on the prediction that reinstatement would not lead to a productive work relationship. Further consideration given to remedy was that the factor of gender was seen as a factor, not the decisive factor, to find liability.

Mr. Justice Leask, for reasons set out below on the judicial review application, disagreed on the findings made by the Tribunal which reduced the lost income award due to the failure of the applicant to accept a return-to-work offer and in so doing determined that the reinstatement submission was to be again reviewed on a second hearing before the Tribunal.[30] This decision was set aside by the Court of Appeal and the Tribunal's decision was restored.

A similar analysis was made in *Wyse v. Coastal Wood Industries*[31] in which case it was determined that reinstatement was not a proper exercise of discretion:

> *After reviewing all of the circumstances, I conclude that reinstatement is not viable in this case. My reasons follow. Mr. Wyse submitted that he should be reinstated to his former position on the green chain, or be given the log deck position or the team captain position. Coastland's witnesses testified that all of these positions required heavy lifting and the green chain requires an employee to be on their feet on a hard floor all day. Mr. Wyse provided no evidence that he was capable of performing these positions. On the contrary, his testimony was that, even by the time of the hearing, he still had to be very careful of his back.*

> *[122] There are other concerns. I accept that Coastland had non-discriminatory performance concerns about Mr. Wyse, including that he had lost interest in his job for reasons not related to his back. It would be inappropriate to place an individual with Mr. Wyse's performance disciplinary history in the team captain position, particularly because both Coastland's management, and the crews that worked with Mr. Wyse, had lost confidence in his willingness to do the job. Also, the parties differed about whether seniority plays a role with respect to Coastland's positions. Regardless of whether this is the case, there was no evidence before me concerning the impact of Mr. Wyse's reinstatement on other workers in the green chain, log deck or team captain positions.*

> *[123] Given these various factors, I am not persuaded that reinstatement is viable in this case and I decline to order it.*

3.4 Alberta

The Alberta statute contains a remedy provision which speaks to the concept of the make whole objective, much like that of British Columbia:

---

30 *J. J. v. School District No. 43 (Coquitlam)*, 2012, accessed September 2014.
  http://www.canlii.org/en/bc/bcsc/doc/2012/2012bcsc523/2012bcsc523.html
31 *Wyse v. Coastal Wood Industries*, 2009, accessed September 2014.
  http://www.canlii.org/en/bc/bchrt/doc/2009/2009bchrt180/2009bchrt180.html

32(1) A human rights tribunal:

(b) may, if it finds that a complaint has merit in whole or in part, order the person against whom the finding was made to do any or all of the following:

... (iii) to make available to the person dealt with contrary to this Act the rights, opportunities or privileges that person was denied contrary to this Act;

The Tribunal in the December 2012 decision of *Cowling v. Her Majesty the Queen in Right of Alberta as represented by Alberta Employment and Immigration*[32] is illustrative of the analysis to determine the propriety of a reinstatement award in a case in which discrimination on account of age was proven. The remedy certainly is not reflexive, but as in the case of British Columbia cases, was exercised as a matter of contextual discretion. The factors considered in *Cowling* included the degree of any ill will from one party to the other, whether the relationship remained viable even through the litigation process, the degree of prejudice to be caused by the requested order and in this case, the apparent benefit to the complainant, given that she remained unemployed:

First, despite the fact that Ms. Cowling was hurt by the actions of Alberta, she does not seem to harbor any ill will to the extent that it would affect her being employed once again for Alberta. Similarly, Alberta's witnesses do not seem to harbor any animosity towards Ms. Cowling by virtue of the litigation. The trust essential in employment relationships does not appear to be irrevocably damaged by this litigation.

[224] Secondly, the evidence indicated that there is currently an opening in the Mediation Services Branch. Ms. Cowling's LRO 3 position was reengineered by the Mediation Services Branch into a management position designated as labour relations advisor after her employment ended in May 2007. The evidence indicates that this position is currently open.

[225] Thirdly, even if there was ill will towards Ms. Cowling in the Mediation Services Branch, the government has a large and varied workforce and there is opportunity for Ms. Cowling to be placed in a setting outside the Mediation Services Branch.

[226] Fourthly, there were no work performance issues with Ms. Cowling. Ms. Cowling received very strong performance assessments.

[227] Lastly, Ms. Cowling continues to be unemployed at the time of the hearing. Every indication is that Ms. Cowling is an excellent candidate to continue to be engaged in the Alberta government workforce. Ms. Cowling is clearly willing, able and very capable of working still today.

---

32 *Cowling v. Her Majesty the Queen in Right of Alberta as represented by Alberta Employment and Immigration*, 2012, accessed September 2014. http://www.canlii.org/en/ab/abhrc/doc/2012/ 2012ahrc12/2012ahrc12.html

As was stated in the decision of *Pitawanakwat* (see footnote 15), one might question the significance of ill will created by the litigation process, given it was the employer's action which gave rise to the need to commence the process.

A similar order had been made in the February 2000 decision of *Weitmann v. City of Calgary Electrical System*,[33] which weighed the significance of the impact of such an order on the applicant's life:

> *Counsel for Mr. Weitmann asked that he be reinstated with the City in a similar position with his seniority intact. Counsel for the Director asked that Mr. Weitmann be reinstated to his former job or a very similar job. Counsel for the City of Calgary submitted that as a result of the panel's decision, the contract with Mr. Weitmann was voidable as of October 16, 1996. As of that date he would be entitled to all rights and benefits available to City of Calgary employees.*

> *Having considered all the evidence the panel orders that Mr. Weitmann be reinstated to employment with the City of Calgary to a position commensurate with his skills, experience and training at a salary level not less than what he received prior to the buyout package.*

> *In reaching this conclusion, the panel took the following factors into account. 1) Mr. Weitmann wants to resume his employment with the City of Calgary, 2) Dr. Cooper testified that Mr. Weitmann's job was the main focus of his life, 3) Mr. Weitmann's loss of employment and the City of Calgary's refusal to consider his request for reconsideration had a negative impact on his mental health which mitigated against his search for alternate employment, 4) Mr. Weitmann had worked for the City of Calgary for 15 years. There is no evidence before this panel that his work was not satisfactory. 5) Dr. Wiseman testified that persons with bipolar disorder could be functional if the disorder was controlled.*

The Alberta Court of Appeal in its recent decision in June 2013 in *AUPE v. Alberta*[34] made note of the reinstatement remedy through the human rights process:

> *[66] It is also relevant that an alternate dispute resolution mechanism, completely divorced from the provisions of the collective agreement and the Code, is available, in the form of a complaint to the Human Rights Commission. That would have provided adjudication by a tribunal with no relationship to the employer. While that alternate process may be less desirable in terms of the time needed to complete, or otherwise, its existence mutes the unfairness argument. Human rights tribunals offer a full range of remedial powers, including that of reinstatement in an employment context ...*

---

33 *Weitmann v. City of Calgary Electrical System*, 2000, accessed September 2014.
   http://www.canlii.org/en/ab/abhrc/doc/2000/2000ahrc1/2000ahrc1.html
34 *AUPE v. Alberta*, 2013, accessed September 2014.
   http://www.canlii.org/en/ab/abca/doc/2013/2013abca212/2013abca212.html

> *[67] While, practically speaking, recourse sought through a human rights complaint may not necessarily result in reinstatement where the employment was time-limited and of relatively short duration, the remedy of damages equivalent to lost wages was alternately available, mirroring the likely result of any successful arbitration had one occurred in these circumstances.*

The comment that reinstatement may not follow where the employment was of short duration is contrary to the *Krieger* reinstatement decision in Ontario and other cases which note the remedy with respect to the make whole concept, in a lost income claim admittedly, is not adversely effected by the length of employment. The issue was not argued before the court in this instance but nonetheless it is instructive of the view taken.

3.5 Saskatchewan

The governing legislation in Saskatchewan provides a specific reference to reinstatement as a remedy which is available, given an adverse finding of liability:

> *Section 31.3 Where the human rights tribunal finds that the complaint to which the inquiry relates is substantiated on the balance of probabilities, the human rights tribunal may, subject to section 31.5, order any person who has contravened any provision of this Act, or any other Act administered by the commission, to do any act or thing that in the opinion of the human rights tribunal constitutes full compliance with that provision and to rectify any injury caused to any person and to make compensation for that injury, including: ...*

> *b) requiring that person to make available to any person injured by that contravention, on the first reasonable occasion, any rights, opportunities or privileges that in the opinion of the human rights tribunal are being or were being denied of the injured person and including, but without restricting the generality of this clause, reinstatement in employment;*

City of Regina v. Kivela is a good example of a claim made under the legislation which led to reinstatement of employment. The case was based on a disability (i.e., cerebral palsy). The disability did not prevent Mr. Kivela, with structural accommodations, from driving a truck. His complaint was based on the failure of the City and his union to allow him to be transferred from a casual employee to permanent status. The first level decision is not reported. The Tribunal found that the complainant would have been awarded a permanent position by the end of 1998 and that the adverse treatment afforded to him had rationalized his decision to cease employment and indeed, sign a resignation letter. An award for lost wages was made for five years from 1999 to 2003 and also the City was ordered to offer re-employment to such a permanent position when one was available. In the interim the clock for lost wages was still running.

The facts are well summarized in the chambers motion which upheld the finding of liability and the award.[35] The Court of Appeal upheld the substance of the decision.[36] Although the appeal of the City raised the issue of the award of reinstatement on appeal, it was seemingly not addressed in argument in a meaningful manner as the appellate court made no comment in this aspect of the decision.

To the same effect is the decision of the Saskatchewan Human Rights Tribunal in *Merrick v. Ipsco Saskatchewan Inc. (No. 3)* 65 CHRR D/220, which allowed for reinstatement having found adverse treatment due to a drug dependency.

3.6 Manitoba

The Manitoba legislation gives similar remedial powers to the Adjudicator:

> *43(2) Where, under subsection (1), the adjudicator decides that a party to the adjudication has contravened this Code, the adjudicator may order the party to do one or more of the following:*
>
> *(a) do or refrain from doing anything in order to secure compliance with this Code, to rectify any circumstance caused by the contravention, or to make just amends for the contravention;*

There are no reported cases dealing with reinstatement applications under the Manitoba legislation.

3.7 New Brunswick

The New Brunswick legislation specifically empowers the human rights tribunal to reinstate:

> *s. 20(6.2) Where, at the conclusion of an inquiry, the Board finds, on a balance of probabilities, that a violation of this Act has occurred, it may order any party found to have violated the Act,*
>
> *(a) to do, or refrain from doing, any act or acts so as to effect compliance with the Act,*
>
> *(b) to rectify any harm caused by the violation,*
>
> *(c) to restore any party adversely affected by the violation to the position he would have been in but for the violation,*
>
> *(d) to reinstate any party who has been removed from a position of employment in violation of the Act.*

The February 2011 decision of the Labour and Employment Board of New Brunswick in *Way v. Department of Education and School District 10*[37] in a case dealing with mandatory retirement at age 65 considered and awarded the remedy of reinstatement.

---

35 *Regina (City) v. Kivela,* 2004, accessed September 2014.
    http://www.canlii.org/en/sk/skqb/doc/2004/2004skqb372/2004skqb372.html
36 *Regina (City) v. Kivela,* 2006, accessed September 2014.
    http://www.canlii.org/en/sk/skca/doc/2006/2006skca38/2006skca38.html
37 *Way v. Department of Education and School District 10,* 2011, accessed September 2014.
    http://www.canlii.org/en/nb/nbleb/doc/2011/2011canlii13074/2011canlii13074.html

The Board noted the absence of any chasm between the parties on a personal level, which presumably would have been a factor in assessing the propriety of reinstatement, as apparently influenced the Board adversely against such an order in the case cited in this passage:

> Here, unlike the case in the Board's decision in A. A. v. New Brunswick (Department of Family and Community Services) [2004] N.B.H.R.B.I.D. No 4 ("A. A."), there is not what the Board finds to be a substantial insult to the dignity of the person concerned, nor are there elevated factors of humiliation or hurt feelings. As Way plainly expressed it himself, "he just hopes to get back driving."

The Tribunal noted in *A.B. v. Brunswick News Inc.*[38] that the "usual remedy" is to allow reinstatement when a violation of the statute has been found, which was not found in this case:

> While reinstatement pursuant to section 20(6.2)(c) is the usual remedy when a Complainant has been terminated in violation of the Act, this Complainant does not seek to return to The Gleaner.
>
> He has retrained as an electrician and he is content to pursue that vocation. He does, however, claim compensation pursuant to section 20(6.2)(f) for the emotional suffering he sustained as a result of the alleged discrimination in the sum of $50,000.00.

3.8 Nova Scotia

The Nova Scotia statutory power of the Board of Inquiry is as follows:

> A board of inquiry may order any party who has contravened this Act to do any act or thing that constitutes full compliance with the Act and to rectify any injury caused to any person or class of persons or to make compensation therefor and, where authorized by and to the extent permitted by the regulations, may make any order against that party, unless that party is the complainant, as to costs as it considers appropriate in the circumstances.

The decision in *McLellan v. MacTara Limited*[39] considered and rejected reinstatement as the proper remedy in the exercise of its discretion. The conclusion noted elsewhere that the remedy of reinstatement should be influenced by the reasoning by which liability has been found. Where the evidence shows that the adverse treatment was a factory as opposed to the factor, such should impact the remedy:

> I have considered and rejected Mr. McLellan's request for reinstatement. I do so for several reasons:
>
> 1. I do not know whether there is a vacant entry position to which to restore Mr. McLellan;
>
> 2. I have already explained that Mr. McLellan's termination was not exclusively the result of physical disability discrimination.

38 *A.B. v. Brunswick News Inc.*< 2009, accessed September 2014.
   http://www.canlii.org/en/nb/nbleb/doc/2009/2009canlii74886/2009canlii74886.html#par60
39 *McLellan v. MacTara Limited*, 2004, accessed September 2014.
   http://www.canlii.org/en/ns/nshrc/doc/2004/2004nshrc4/2004nshrc4.html#par67

He was terminated with notice;

3. *The passage of time has been lengthy and the workplace adjustments at MacTara since would mean that a reinstatement order could unintentionally privilege Mr. McLellan above other longer term MacTara employees who today remain on layoff;*

4. *Mr. McLellan doubts that reinstatement would be a positive experience for himself;*

5. *I do not believe that it would benefit the public interest, or serve any instructive purpose for MacTara, in any way.*

3.9 Newfoundland and Labrador

The Newfoundland and Labrador statute provides for relief allowing for a reinstatement remedy:

39. (1) A board of inquiry

(b) *may, where it finds that a complaint is justified in whole or in part, order the person against whom the finding was made to do one or more of the following: ...*

(iii) *to make available to the person discriminated against the rights, opportunities, or privileges he or she was denied contrary to this Act.*

There are not any reported cases dealing with the issue of reinstatement.

3.10 Prince Edward Island

The Prince Edward Island legislation provides specifically for a reinstatement remedy:

28.4 (1) A Human Rights Panel

(b) *subject to subsection (2), may, if it finds that a complaint has merit in whole or in part, order the person against whom the finding was made to do any or all of the following: ...*

(iii) *to make available to the complainant or other person dealt with contrary to this Act, the rights, opportunities, or privileges that the person was denied contrary to this Act;*

The human rights panel in its June 2010 decision in *Nilsson v. University of Prince Edward Island* agreed with the words of Wilson J., referenced in her dissenting opinion in McKinney[40] and in a similar age discrimination case, determined that reinstatement was the correct remedy:

The fact that the Complainants are over the age of 65 and, given the nature of their employment, the Panel finds that it would be

---

40 *McKinney v. University of Guelph*, 1990, accessed September 2014.
   http://www.canlii.org/en/ca/scc/doc/1990/1990canlii60/1990canlii60.html

unlikely for the Complainants to find similar employment. Accordingly, the Panel considers reinstatement to be an appropriate remedy in the circumstances. Pursuant to s. 28.4(1)(b)(v) of the Act, the Panel orders the University to reinstate Dr. Nilsson and Dr. Wills to their former positions with tenure. The Panel orders the University to reinstate Ms. Fell to a position comparable to the position she held prior to the termination of her employment.

3.11 Yukon

The *Yukon Human Rights Act* does not specifically empower reinstatement but allows for the Board to "rectify any condition that causes the discrimination" which presumably includes reinstatement as the later statutory qualifier prohibits the loss of employment of any person who had accepted such employment in good faith.

> *If complaint established*
>
> *24(1) If the complaint is proven on the balance of probabilities, the board of adjudication may order the party who discriminated to ...*
>
> > *(b)   rectify any condition that causes the discrimination;*
>
> *(2) No order made under this section shall contain a term*
>
> > *(a)   requiring an individual to be removed from employment if the individual accepted the position in good faith;*

The Yukon Human Rights Board of Adjudication in its December 2008 decision of *Hayes v. Yukon College 67* CHRR D/408 (Evans, Tkachuk and Riseborough) found liability against the respondent due to its adverse treatment of the applicant who suffered from a debilitating liver disease. An order of reinstatement was made even when the applicant was unable to return to active employment.

3.12 Northwest Territories

A similar Northwest Territories legislative provision allows the Board to order reinstatement:

> *(3)   If the adjudicator finds, under subsection (1), that a complaint has merit in whole or in part, the adjudicator (a) may order a party against whom the finding was made to do one or more of the following: ...*
>
> > *(iii)   to make available to any party dealt with contrary to this Act the rights, opportunities or privileges that the person was denied contrary to this Act ...*

There are no reported cases dealing with reinstatement under any of the human rights statutes for the Northwest Territories.

3.13 Nunavut

In Nunavut the *Human Rights Act* also allows for reinstatement, given a finding of liability:

> *(3) If the Tribunal finds, under subsection (1), that a notification has merit in whole or in part, the Tribunal*
>
> *(a) may order a party against whom the finding was made to do one or more of the following: ...*
>
> > *(iii) to make available to any party dealt with contrary to this Act or the regulations, the rights, opportunities or privilege that the person was denied contrary to this Act or the regulations ...*

There are no reported cases dealing with reinstatement under any of the human rights statutes for Nunavut.

8
Duty to Mitigate Income Loss

Mitigation simply means taking steps to minimize the loss, which in the case of a lost income claim, translates into looking for comparable employment. As a general rule, the employee remains under an obligation to take reasonable steps to seek comparable employment, as is the case in common-law wrongful dismissal actions.

There is some discussion which follows as to whose duty it is to show mitigation. Does the employee need to show he or she has taken all reasonable steps to look for other employment? Or does the employer need to prove the opposite, that is, the employee has failed to conduct a proper job search?

The case law favours that the employer has the "onus" to show the employee has failed to do a reasonable job search as well as had the employee done so, he or she could have found a new job.

My view is that you, as a complainant, should not fool around with this. Be prepared for the worst and show that you have taken all reasonable steps to find a new job. Keep records and show you were active.

As in common-law cases, the onus to prove a failure to mitigate is on the employer. As was found in *Payette v. Alarm Guard Service:*[1]

---

1   *Payette v. Alarm Guard Service*, 2011, accessed September 2014.
    http://www.canlii.org/en/on/onhrt/doc/2011/2011hrto109/2011hrto109.html

[36] The applicant is under a duty to mitigate her losses by making reasonable efforts to obtain suitable employment, and is only entitled to be compensated for those losses that could not have been avoided. However, the respondents have the onus of proving the applicant's failure to mitigate.

The Supreme Court of Canada in the common-law cases has defined the onus on the employer as twofold. The employer must show a breach of the obligation and must then introduce affirmative evidence to show that had the employee taken reasonable steps to seek employment, success likely would have followed. The leading cases on this subject are *Red Deer College v. Michaels*[2] and *Evans v. Teamsters Local Union No. 31.*[3]

This issue was addressed in the Prince Edward Island Human Rights Tribunal decision of *Matheson v. Presbytery of Prince Edward Island,*[4] holding that the onus should be that of the double barrel variety as set out in *Red Deer College*:

> *58. The Supreme Court of Canada in Red Deer College v. Michaels, 1975 CanLII 15 (SCC), [1976] 2 S.C.R. 324, held that the onus falls on the defendant to prove that an employee has failed to take reasonable steps to mitigate his losses. This principle has been supported by numerous decisions, including Morgan v. Canada (Armed Forces) (1991)13 C.H.R.R. D/42. The onus has also been succinctly described in Levitt on the Law of Dismissal in Canada, at p. 234 as follows:*
>
>> *The onus is on the employer to prove, first failure to mitigate on the employee's part and, secondly, that the employee would have found another comparable position if one had been searched for*

All this means that a Human Rights Tribunal need not necessarily apply the usual law on mitigation, although 99 times out of a 100, it does just that.

The BC Supreme Court decision in *McIntosh v. Metro Aluminum Products Ltd.*[5] sat on a judicial review of a Human Rights Tribunal decision which did not apply the onus as in *Red Deer* and *Evans*. The Court determined that Section 37 of relevant Code gave discretion to the Tribunal to order compensation for "all, or a part" of the lost wages.

It was asserted on review that the Tribunal made a legal error in not applying common-law mitigation principles of mitigation, a decision which the Court determined that the Tribunal was entitled to make and that there was no legal obligation to apply the onus as set out in the Supreme Court decisions of *Red Deer* and *Evans*.

---

2   *Red Deer College v. Michaels*, 1976, accessed September 2014.
    http://www.canlii.org/en/ca/scc/doc/1975/1975canlii15/1975canlii15.htm
3   *Evans v. Teamsters Local Union No. 31*, 2008, accessed September 2014.
    http://www.canlii.org/en/ca/scc/doc/2008/2008scc20/2008scc20.html
4   *Matheson v. Presbytery of Prince Edward Island*, 2007, accessed September 2014.
    http://www.canlii.org/en/pe/peihrc/doc/2007/2007canlii60951/2007canlii60951.html
5   *McIntosh v. Metro Aluminum Products Ltd.*, 2012, accessed September 2014.
    http://www.canlii.org/en/bc/bcsc/doc/2012/2012bcsc345/2012bcsc345.html#par52

The claimant had argued, unsuccessfully, that the mitigation obligation of the Supreme Court of Canada decisions required the employer to prove a two-step process, such being a failure to mitigate, followed by employer evidence that had there been an active job search, there would have been positive results likely to ensue.

> It is apparent to me that the Tribunal took into account the legal onus on the respondents to prove a failure of the petitioner to mitigate her loss by identifying any available position she declined or failed to pursue (para. 145). It is equally clear the Tribunal took into account all the evidence before it when it made its decision on wage loss stating, "However, in exercising my remedial discretion under the Code, I am entitled to take into consideration all of the evidence properly before me, including the extent of Ms. McIntosh's job search efforts, and I have done so." (para. 146). The Tribunal went on to conclude, based on the evidence, that "up until October, Ms. McIntosh's job search does not seem particularly diligent." (para. 147).

> [48] While the principles set out in Red Deer have been applied universally by courts in Canada (as demonstrated by the number of authorities cited by the petitioner in her Brief of Authorities) it must be remembered that case and the cases referred to by the petitioner arise from a breach of contract or a "wrongful dismissal."

> [49] The present case arises in an administrative law context. Section 37 of the Code is a remedial section which gives a discretion to the Tribunal to make an order that compensates for "all, or a part" of the wages lost. Based on the language of s. 37, the Tribunal was entitled to assess all the evidence before it in making that determination, including the efforts of the petitioner to find alternate employment as expounded by her. The fact other panels may have applied Red Deer and Evans in assisting them determine how much of the wage loss to award does not prevent a Tribunal member from departing from past decisions.

The Federal Court of Appeal in its 2007 decision of *Chopra v. Canada (Attorney General)*[6] reviewed the decision of the Tribunal in which a finding had been made that the complainant had failed to take reasonable steps to mitigate his damage claim. The complaint was based on ethnic origin. The Court of Appeal concluded that the Tribunal was not mandated to apply the concept of mitigation but may do so in the exercise of its discretion.

The Alberta Court of Appeal in *Walsh v. Mobil Oil Canada*[7] stated that in human rights cases, different considerations in reviewing the mitigation obligation may apply and to this end offered the example of the impact on a complainant of the consequences of suffering from a toxic work relationship caused presumably by a human rights violation:

---

6 *Chopra v. Canada (Attorney General)*, 2007, accessed September 2014.
   http://www.canlii.org/en/ca/fca/doc/2007/2007fca268/2007fca268.html
7 *Walsh v. Mobil Oil Canada*, 2013, accessed September 2014.
   http://www.canlii.org/en/ab/abca/doc/2013/2013abca238/2013abca238.html

However, additional considerations come into play when the concept of mitigation is applied in the discrimination context. For example, a tribunal should take into consideration the after-effects of exposure to a poisoned work environment in looking at the duty to mitigate: Holness v. South Alder Farms Ltd. (1999) CHRR Doc. 99-019 (BCHRT).

How far down the field this analysis pushes the ball is highly debatable. At the end of the day, it would appear there has been no dramatic revision to the traditional view that mitigation is the order of the day. The following is from the Alberta Court of Appeal in *Walsh*:

The most that can be said is that tribunals have drawn from contract and tort law, particularly by importing the need for a causal link and the duty to mitigate, to ascertain the amount and extent of wage loss damages sustained as a result of discriminatory conduct.

A fair synthesis may be that the Tribunal will look to mitigation as the usual requirement but has considerable latitude in its discretion as to whether this obligation has been fulfilled and is not bound by traditional common-law concepts. To the same end is the conclusion reached by the British Columbia the Court of Appeal discussed subsequently on the application of the *Evans* concept in *J.J. v. School District 43 (Coquitlam)*.[8]

1. Provide Medical Evidence

If you are arguing that you could not do a proper job search because you were medically unable to do so, then you should prove this by a medical report.

Payette v. Alarm Guard Security Service (see footnote 1) is an example of a case in which the Tribunal found that the complainant had failed in her obligation to take reasonable steps to mitigate her income loss. No details of a job search were provided. Although the complainant asserted her emotional state prevented an active job search, there was no medical evidence to demonstrate the degree of the severity of this condition.

Accordingly, even though the onus of asserting a failure to mitigate rests on the employer, when the complainant alleges a medical condition prevents an ongoing job search, the obligation to adduce proper supporting medical evidence is that of the complainant. This issue was again reviewed in *Turner v. 507638 Ontario*.[9]

The duty to mitigate is to act reasonably. It is clear that the court will consider the individual circumstances of the complainant and should she be troubled by physical or emotional ailments making it difficult for her to seek employment, this should not be weighed against her, as was confirmed by the Alberta Court of Appeal in *Walsh v. Mobil Oil Canada* (see footnote 7):

8 *J.J. v. School District 43 (Coquitlam)*, 2013, accessed September 2014.
    http://www.canlii.org/en/bc/bcca/doc/2013/2013bcca67/2013bcca67.html#par37
9 *Turner v. 507638 Ontario*, 2009, accessed September 2014.
    http://www.canlii.org/en/on/onhrt/doc/2009/2009hrto249/2009hrto249.html

While it is true that Ms. Walsh has a duty to mitigate that loss and take reasonable steps to find alternate employment she is only required to act reasonably. Any delay in mitigation because of physical, mental, or emotional problems arising from her experience with Mobil should be taken into account. If her injuries as a result of the accident caused her problems in seeking work elsewhere, she is entitled to be compensated. If, as a result of emotional or mental anguish, she was prevented from seeking alternate employment, again she is only obligated to act reasonably. If she does so, she is entitled to compensation for whatever time she is off work.

The accident referenced in the text here was a car accident which was not work related. This passage is from a first-level review of the Tribunal decision and not the final appellate decision which did uphold the claim awarded for the income loss, but did not specifically endorse these words.

The passage immediately above was endorsed by the Human Rights Tribunal in *Munoz v. Diocese of Toronto*[10] in 2011 before the Court of Appeal decision in *Walsh*.

2. Emotional Trauma Considerations

In *Dubé v. CTS Career College*[11] a Tribunal decision in August of 2010 did consider the impact of the emotional trauma suffered by the complainant. It saw this as a factor in assessing the reasonableness of the complainant's job search efforts.

[20] Furthermore, the applicant's evidence was that, emotionally, he "bottomed out" as a result of the respondent's discriminatory treatment. While he was not idle, he was not always consistent in his job search. The question for the Tribunal is whether the respondent has established that the applicant's efforts were not reasonable. Boards and Tribunals have recognized that the experience of discrimination can affect victims' ability to seek alternative employment, or otherwise mitigate their losses: see Almeida v. Chubb Fire Security Division (1984), 5 C.H.R.R. D/2104 (Ont. Bd. Inq.). The evidence summarized in the Decision makes clear my finding that the applicant was both distraught by the discrimination, and developed serious and understandable doubts that he would ever be able to emerge from the shadow of his past. While these factors did not relieve him of the duty to mitigate, they inform the analysis of what is reasonable in the circumstances.

3. Impact of a Finding of Failure to Mitigate

If the Tribunal finds that you have failed to look for a job that does not mean your claim is zero. Where there has been a finding of a failure to mitigate, the Tribunal may assess what a fair time period to find other

10 *Munoz v. Diocese of Toronto*, 2011, accessed September 2014.
   http://www.canlii.org/en/on/onhrt/doc/2011/2011hrto1434/2011hrto1434.html
11 *Dubé v. CTS Career College*, 2010, accessed September 2014.
   http://www.canlii.org/en/on/onhrt/doc/2010/2010hrto1694/2010hrto1694.html

employment would have been and use this conclusion for the assessment of the income loss. Such was the result in *Adams v. Knoll North America*:[12]

> *[21] Upon finding the applicant failed to mitigate his losses, I must determine how long it likely would have taken for him to find another job had he tried to do so. There is no question that it would have taken the applicant some time. This represents his "unavoidable loss" and it is this loss that the respondent is responsible for. In the circumstances of this case, I find that it would have taken the applicant three months to find another job. I recognize that this is a somewhat arbitrary determination. However, in light of the applicant's age, work history, and the economy in March 2008, it is a reasonable period of time.*
>
> *[22] I therefore find that the applicant is entitled lost wages for the period March 4, 2008 to June 4, 2008 in the amount of $10,301.40. The applicant is also entitled to his health and dental benefits during this period at a reimbursement rate of eighty percent. This entitles the applicant to an additional amount of $216.28. The applicant is not entitled to vacation pay because I find he would have taken his vacation during his employment. Similarly, the applicant is not entitled to a bonus or safety shoes because there is no evidence that he consistently received a bonus or that he was reimbursed for safety shoes on a yearly basis.*

If your company offers you your job back and you have refused to take it, while this may altogether mean reinstatement is impossible, it may also impact your claim for lost income to the date of this offer. It may depend on the terms surrounding the offer, such as a condition to give up the case. The precise details would need to be examined.

Occasionally arguments may arise by which the employer may assert that the applicant had an obligation to return to work based on an offer made of comparable employment following dismissal or an alleged dismissal.

Many have said that the leading case on the mitigation obligation in an employment context is the 2008 Supreme Court of Canada decision in *Evans v. Teamsters Local Union No. 31* (see footnote 3). In reality it added only one new wrinkle. The fundamental principles of mitigation were in place years before this decision and repeated once again. It did deal with the new concept of considering the obligation of a dismissed employee to return to work at the request of the employer following a termination. This was the only new principle in dealing with this.

The majority of the Supreme Court of Canada determined that in certain circumstances, it will be necessary for the dismissed employee to return to the employ of the company when an offer of alternate employment has been extended. This being said, it remains the employer's onus to show a failure to mitigate in this circumstance.

---

12 *Adams v. Knoll North America*, 2010, accessed September 2014.
   http://www.canlii.org/en/on/onhrt/doc/2010/2010hrto376/2010hrto376.html

The Court noted that the analysis is contextual and multifactored. The critical issue is that the employee not be obliged to mitigate by working in "an atmosphere of hostility, embarrassment, or humiliation," a standard which is to be reviewed objectively. This being stated, the non-tangible elements including "work atmosphere, stigma, and loss of dignity" in addition to the tangible elements are to be included in the evaluation.

The British Columbia Human Rights Tribunal in *J.J. v. School District No. 43 (No. 5)*[13] considered and applied the *Evans* principle of mitigation in determining the applicant's loss of income claim. The employer had agreed to re-employ the applicant on terms which the complainant found unacceptable and which the Tribunal found reasonable and non-discriminatory. At the time this offer was made, the complainant was seeking employment with the District School Board. Her claim for lost income was accordingly adversely affected:

> *J.J. has the responsibility of mitigating any wage loss. In April 2006, the District agreed to re-hire J.J. in her temporary casual position if she agreed to a number of terms. In particular, and as noted above, she was required to acknowledge that: her employment was on a temporary (or seasonal) casual basis, and that there was no guarantee of employment for subsequent years; that seniority was only for the current period of employment and did not carry over from year to year; and that no supervisory duties would be assigned to seasonal employees.*

In this issue, the chambers justice, Mr. Justice Leask, expressed disagreement and concluded that the Tribunal did not apply *Evans* correctly by failing to reflect on the context of the employment relationship and hence set aside the wage reduction based on the application of *Evans*. On further review by the Court of Appeal (see footnote 8), this court determined that the Tribunal was not mandated to apply the common-law concept of mitigation in assessing the income loss. The Court of Appeal concluded that the Tribunal's decision, whether or not it chose to apply *Evans*, was a discretionary one and could not be challenged on judicial review. For this reason, in part, the chambers decision was set aside and that of the Tribunal restored.

An early decision dealing with the obligation to accept an alternative offer of employment from the same employer was the decision of *Rand and Canadian Union of Industrial Employees v. Sealy Eastern Limited, Upholstery Division* (Cumming) 3 CHRR D/938. Rand was terminated from his position as a maintenance mechanic due to his refusal to work on the Sabbath and was ordered to be reinstated. The employer had offered to him alternative employment as a "springer" or "packer" following the dispute. The "springer" position was seen to be overly physically demanding, but the "packer" position was a job Rand could have performed but chose not to, as it was a Grade 5 level position, compared to that of the mechanic which was a Grade 17 and paid 42 percent less than the more senior position. The

13 *J.J. v. School District No. 43 (No. 5)*, 2008, accessed September 2014.
   http://www.canlii.org/en/bc/bchrt/doc/2008/2008bchrt360/2008bchrt360.html

packer position was accompanied by production bonuses which may have allowed Rand an income which was approximate to his prior income level or even exceeded it, as was found.

The Board found that Rand could have worked in this position without waiving his right under the Code to seek the remedy in question. The Board concluded that Rand ought to have accepted this position until the hearing took place or until such time that he found other employment. The claim for lost income was denied.

4. Mitigation Expenses

Generally speaking, all reasonable job search expenses should be recoverable. You should document your search by keeping receipts and be able to explain why the expenses were job-search related. Ontario uses a rate of 25 cents per kilometre in the rules of court practice which should follow in the Human Rights Tribunal as well.

A successful claim for mitigation expenses was made in *Xu v. The Ottawa Hospital*.[14] The complainant was awarded additional travel costs incurred in her new position of employment for the time period of October 1, 2009, her last active date of employment, through to July 2010.

5. Employment Insurance Benefits

You may apply for Employment Insurance (EI) benefits following termination of employment. A claim for lost income against the employer will not be reduced by EI benefits.

The *Employment Insurance Act* requires that any sums received by you as a consequence of termination of employment will cause a repayment obligation. The sum received is allocated as equal to normal weekly earnings. This will include any sum recovered for employment-related benefits.

The lost income claim that you received will be insurable earnings. For example, if you recover nine months of lost income, triggering a repayment obligation and you remained unemployed after that time period, you will be able to make a new claim for benefits.

Certain payments are not considered earnings. If your case is settled or proceeds to a hearing, the onus is on you to show that any sum received is not earnings and not subject to a repayment obligation. Sums that may have been received for unpaid wages owing as of termination date, moving expenses, retraining costs, relocation, and counseling fees are not earnings.

If you have asserted a reinstatement claim and have accepted a payment in lieu of this right, the sum received will not be considered earnings. You must be able to show that the right of reinstatement existed by federal,

---

14 *Xu v. The Ottawa Hospital*, 2012, accessed September 2014.
http://www.canlii.org/en/on/onhrt/doc/2012/2012hrto337/2012hrto337.html

provincial, or territorial statute or collective agreement; that the remedy was asserted; and that the sum received was compensation for relinquishing the right to reinstatement. That is one reason why it is important to put the reinstatement claim in your initial claim.

Similarly your claim made for damages for loss of dignity and emotional distress will not give rise to a repayment obligation or, for that matter, to income tax. Punitive damages also are not earnings and not subject to a repayment obligation.

If you settle the case, the minutes of settlement should clearly address the allocation of settlement funds.

Given that the claims are also non-taxable payments, the benefits of these allocations and appropriate planning and evidence to support are evident.

9
Duty of the Employer to Investigate

Duty of the employer to investigate is an important topic in Ontario. If the company ignores an employee's complaint, he or she can still win a damage award for injured feelings, even if the main claim fails. The sum awarded tends to be in the range of $5,000 to $7,500.

Under the Ontario Code, an employer may be held liable for the way in which it responds to a complaint of a violation of the Code. The theory behind the imposition of this obligation is an attempt to ensure that the rights created by the Code are meaningful.

1. Conduct Required to Trigger the Duty to Investigate

The duty to investigate arises once the complainant has made known the allegations of a Code violation. As was stated in *Frolov v. Mosregion Investment Corporation:*[1]

> *Once the applicant brought issues of sexual harassment/solicitation to the attention of the respondent, the respondent had an obligation under the Code to respond reasonably and adequately to*

---

1 *Frolov v. Mosregion Investment Corporation*, 2010, accessed September 2014. http://www.canlii.org/en/on/onhrt/doc/2010/2010hrto1789/2010hrto1789.html#par84

the applicant's complaints. It failed to do so and thus became liable under the Code for its inadequate response.

2. A Reasonable Investigation

The duty of the employer is to conduct a reasonable investigation as opposed to a perfect one. In *Laskowska v. Marineland of Canada Inc.*,[2] the Tribunal determined the following tests to assess the conduct of the employer in replying to the internal complaint:

> *(1) Awareness of issues of discrimination/harassment, Policy Complaint Mechanism and Training: Was there an awareness of issues of discrimination and harassment in the workplace at the time of the incident? Was there a suitable anti-discrimination/harassment policy? Was there a proper complaint mechanism in place? Was adequate training given to management and employees;*

> *(2) Post-Complaint: Seriousness, Promptness, Taking Care of its Employee, Investigation and Action: Once an internal complaint was made, did the employer treat it seriously? Did it deal with the matter promptly and sensitively? Did it reasonably investigate and act?; and*

> *(3) Resolution of the Complaint (including providing the Complainant with a Healthy Work Environment) and Communication: Did the employer provide a reasonable resolution in the circumstances? If the complainant chose to return to work, could the employer provide him/her with a healthy, discrimination-free work environment? Did it communicate its findings and actions to the complainant?*

The Tribunal in *Laskowska* continued to state that the employer need not necessarily touch all the bases in every case, although such would be considered the exception. The overall question to be answered is: Did the employer, given all the circumstances, act reasonably?

> *While the above three elements are of a general nature, their application must retain some flexibility to take into account the unique facts of each case. The standard is one of reasonableness, not correctness or perfection. There may have been several options — all reasonable — open to the employer. The employer need not satisfy each element in every case in order to be judged to have acted reasonably, although that would be the exception rather than the norm. One must look at each element individually and then in the aggregate before passing judgment on whether the employer acted reasonably.*

It is essential to the investigative process that the employer shows neutrality and lack of bias to both sides of the dispute. As was stated in *Murchie v. JB's Mongolian Grill:*[3]

2 *Laskowska v. Marineland of Canada Inc.*, 2005, accessed September 2014.
   http://www.canlii.org/en/on/onhrt/doc/2005/2005hrto30/2005hrto30.html
3 *Murchie v. JB's Mongolian Grill*, 2006, accessed September 2014.
   http://www.canlii.org/en/on/onhrt/doc/2006/2006hrto33/2006hrto33.html#_ftn1

Subsection 5(1) of the Code provides that "Every person has a right to equal treatment with respect to employment without discrimination because of ... sex." The Tribunal and the courts have included in that right, such things as the right to a discrimination-free environment, or a non-poisoned workplace, even though it does not explicitly state that in the concisely worded general anti-discrimination provision of s.5 (1). From that general workplace anti-discrimination clause flows other obligations, such as the "duty not to condone or further a discriminatory act that has already occurred" (see Payne) and the duty on an employer to investigate a complaint of discrimination....

Human rights jurisprudence has established that an employer is under a duty to take reasonable steps to address allegations of discrimination in the workplace, and that a failure to do so will itself result in liability under the Code ...

It would make the protection under s.5(1) to a discrimination-free work environment a hollow one if an employer could sit idly when a complaint of discrimination was made and not have to investigate it. If that were so, how could it determine if a discriminatory act occurred or a poisoned work environment existed? The duty to investigate is a "means" by which the employer ensures that it is achieving the Code-mandated "ends" of operating in a discrimination-free environment and providing its employees with a safe work environment.

In *Nelson v. Lakehead University*[4] the employer was also found to be in violation of its obligation to investigate the complaint fairly. Liability was found on this ground and the substantive complaint, which was based on age discrimination was dismissed. The employer's response to the complaint was determined to be dismissive and did not show reasonable steps to investigate the complaint.

The Supreme Court of Canada came to a similar conclusion in its 1987 decision of *Robichaud v. Canada (Treasury Board)*.[5] The Court stated that an employer which responds quickly to a complaint by developing a scheme to remedy and address recurrence of a human rights violation will not be liable to the same extent as one which fails to address such issues.

A parallel conclusion was reached in *Payette v. Alarm Guard Security Service*.[6] No investigation was undertaken to determine the validity of the complaint. The reasonableness of the employer's response, the presence of an anti-harassment policy, and a related investigative process were all seen as relevant to the determination on remedy.

2.1 Wall test

The wall test was stated as follows:

---

4 *Nelson v. Lakehead University*, 2008, accessed September 2014.
   http://www.canlii.org/en/on/onhrt/doc/2008/2008hrto41/2008hrto41.html
5 *Robichaud v. Canada (Treasury Board)*, 1987, accessed September 2014.
   http://www.canlii.org/en/ca/scc/doc/1987/1987canlii73/1987canlii73.html
6 *Payette v. Alarm Guard Security Service*, 2011, accessed September 2014.
   http://www.canlii.org/en/on/onhrt/doc/2011/2011hrto109/2011hrto109.html

There are six elements to the "Wall" test used to assess the reasonableness of the employer's response, see: Wall v. University of Waterloo (1990) 27 C.H.R.R. D/44 (Ont. Bd. Inq.), at paragraph 160, which are summarized as follows:

- *There is an obligation of promptness in dealing with a harassment complaint.*

- *There is an awareness by the employer that sexual harassment is prohibited conduct.*

- *The issue must be dealt with seriously.*

- *The employer must demonstrate that there is a complaint mechanism in place.*

- *The employer has an obligation to provide a healthy work environment.*

- *There is an obligation for management to communicate its actions to a complainant.*

[40] The corporate respondent also failed to investigate at any time after it was served with the underlying complaint filed with the Commission in 2007. In my view, such a failure to reasonably investigate exacerbated and compounded the infringement of the applicant's right to be free from harassment on the basis of sex and sexual solicitation. Since there is no dispute that Mr. Ameri was an employee, during the relevant time, I am satisfied the corporate respondent is liable for the failure to investigate under section 46.3 of the Code and in the circumstances of this case.

In this case, a separate award was made of $5,000 due to the failure of the corporation to investigate the complaint. This also adversely affected the credibility of the company's defence.

2.2 Immediate investigation may reduce victim's harm

The Tribunal in *Harriott v. National Money Mart*,[7] made a similar finding of a failure to properly investigate the complaint of Ms. Harriott. One reason to put into place an immediate investigation is to minimize the harm suffered by the victim, as the Tribunal determined:

[147] It is clear that the responsible District Manager, Ms. O'Neil, was advised on a number of occasions by a number of different people that Mr. Wade's conduct in the workplace was inappropriate and likely constituted sexual harassment. Despite that, she was either unwilling or unable to initiate an investigation in response to these complaints. The result was that the time frame within which the applicant suffered sexual harassment at the hands of Mr. Wade was elongated beyond what it likely would have been

---

7   *Harriott v. National Money Mart*, 2010, accessed September 2014.
   http://www.canlii.org/en/on/onhrt/doc/2010/2010hrto353/2010hrto353.html

had Ms. O'Neil acted promptly upon receipt of the first or second complaint about Mr. Wade. The law imposes an obligation on employers to promptly investigate sexual harassment for a reason: to minimize the length of time that the victim of the harassment is required to endure the harassment.

[148] I have also found that the company's investigation in response to the applicant's harassment complaint was inadequate in a number of respects. It also was more prolonged than it needed to be, and the fact that the company failed to keep the applicant apprised of the status of the investigation or its outcome added to her stress.

A total award was made of $30,000 inclusive of the damages attributed to the failure to investigate of $7,500.

The Tribunal in *Barfi-Kwabeno v. Knoll North America Corporation*[8] agreed with the obligation, questioned the employer's conduct, but found no violation on the facts before it showing a violation of the obligation to conduct a reasonable investigation:

It is undisputed the applicant made two statements about race in the course of the employer's investigation of the October 22, 2004 incident. The notes of his interview with Khesh Pershad record that the applicant said, "I will not run a defective product. Knoll does not care if the life of a Black Man is lost." Ms. Blahitka testified that during a meeting on October 26, the applicant said that he was a black man in the workplace, that his safety was not guaranteed and that he wanted his safety to be guaranteed. She says she replied that the employer did not tolerate discrimination in the workplace and if he had those concerns, the company would deal with them when he returned to work.

[17] The Tribunal has held that there is duty under the Code to take reasonable steps to investigate allegations of discrimination ...

[18] I must admit to some concern about the employer's failure to ask Mr. Barfi-Kwabena further questions to ascertain what he meant by these statements. However, viewed in context, I find that these statements did not trigger a duty on the employer to carry out any further investigations. The statements that Knoll did not care about the safety of a black man and would not guarantee the safety of a black man in the workplace must be seen in the context of the dispute between the applicant and Knoll about the safety of the mack wrapper machine. The reasonable interpretation of these assertions, given the events that had taken place, were that Knoll had responded to his safety concerns as it had because of his race. There had been extensive steps taken to deal with those concerns, including a meeting, action plan, and an investigation by the Ministry of Labour. The machine appeared to be safe. There were no further steps that were reasonably necessary to deal with

---

8   *Barfi-Kwabeno v. Knoll North America Corporation*, 2009, accessed September 2014. http://www.canlii.org/en/on/onhrt/doc/2009/2009hrto619/2009hrto619.html

> *the applicant's allegations when his safety concerns had been addressed. The analysis of the need to investigate allegations about risks to the "safety of a black man" would be completely different if they did not come in the context of a dispute about the safety of workplace equipment.*
>
> *[19] I therefore find that there was no violation of the Code through the employer's failure to conduct further investigation as a result of Mr. Barfi-Kwabena's statements.*

This liability on the employer may be found, even though a substantive violation of the Code has not been proven. For example, in *Frolov v. Mosregion Investment Corporation* (see footnote 1) the complainant was male, who asserted a female was sexually harassing him. The employer did not act when made aware of the complaint, its defence being that it was unaware that men could experience sexual harassment:

> *In this case, the alleged victim was a man claiming that a woman was sexually harassing or soliciting him. Mr. Bakouchev failed to act upon the applicant's initial allegations and his first written complaint. While the respondent may not have been aware that men can experience sexual harassment or is unaware of the different types of sexual harassment that can exist, this does not eliminate the respondent's obligation to investigate into the applicant's allegations. The Tribunal has held that a respondent's ignorance about its Code obligations does not excuse the respondent or act as a defence to its Code obligations.*

Liability was accordingly found for the independent failure to conduct an investigation.

> *Once the applicant brought issues of sexual harassment/solicitation to the attention of the respondent, the respondent had an obligation under the Code to respond reasonably and adequately to the applicant's complaints. It failed to do so and thus became liable under the Code for its inadequate response.*

The employer's response to the complaint was "stop complaining," "be a reasonable man," and "you should be pleased that she pays attention to you." This conduct was found to be in violation of section 5(1) of the Code and constituted discrimination on the basis of gender. There was no finding of sexual harassment or solicitation. The award was based solely on the failure to conduct a proper investigation:

> *As I have set out earlier in this Decision, I cannot make any findings about whether the applicant was sexually harassed or sexually solicited by the co-worker and thus am not awarding any remedies with respect to that issue. I have determined that the respondent discriminated against the applicant on the basis of gender (sex) and failed to reasonably investigate into the applicant's written complaints about the co-worker's conduct and thus has violated the Code.*

[106] The applicant testified about his experience of victimization. He testified that he felt that there was nothing he could do to have his concerns addressed and nowhere for him to turn except to file his Application. The failure of the respondent to investigate into his concerns affected his family relationships, his work, and his work relationships. This was compounded when the respondent commenced an investigation, not from the perspective of a man alleging harassment by a woman, but a woman alleging harassment by a man.

[107] Some of the Tribunal's more recent decisions, in which there were findings of sexual harassment and/or sexual solicitation as well as job loss, as well as a failure to investigate, have awarded monetary compensation over $20,000, in addition to other monetary remedies, for violation of the applicant's inherent right to be free from discrimination and harassment. See, for example, Smith, supra, at para. 187 and Harriott, supra, at para. 156.

[108] In the circumstances of this case, and in light of the fact that I am making no findings that sexual harassment and/or solicitation occurred, I find it appropriate to award $7,500 for the violation of the applicant's inherent right to be free from discrimination and harassment and for the respondent's failure to reasonably investigate. In awarding this amount, I have considered the fact that the applicant did not lose his job and was not in a vulnerable position in that the allegations were about his subordinate. I have also considered that the applicant raised serious issues about the co-worker in writing on three occasions before the respondent started an investigation, which, for the reasons described above, was flawed.

3. Damage Awards for Failure to Investigate

The range of damage awards in Ontario for a finding of failure to investigate tends to be in the range of $5,000 to $7,500. Two examples include:

- *Payette v. Alarm Guard Security Service (see footnote 6) allowed the sum of $5,000 for failure to investigate the complaint.*

- *Selinger v. McFarland*[9] *found the employer in violation of its obligation to investigate the complaint and awarded the sum of $7,000 as damages for this violation.*

A failure to make a proper response was found in *Sutton v. Jarvis Ryan Associates*[10] but no financial compensation was ordered, which appeared to be influenced by a finding of no liability on the substantive complaints, a conclusion which is contrary to the reasoning of prior and subsequent decisions.

---

9 *Selinger v. McFarland*, 2008, accessed September 2014.
   http://www.canlii.org/en/on/onhrt/doc/2008/2008hrto49/2008hrto49.html
10 *Sutton v. Jarvis Ryan Associates*, 2010, accessed September 2014.
   http://www.canlii.org/en/on/onhrt/doc/2010/2010hrto2421/2010hrto2421.html

Other jurisdictions across Canada do not allow for such an independent award although the need to conduct a proper investigation of the complaint is well founded. For example, the Alberta Court of Queen's Bench noted in *Kinch v. Amoco* the need to do so:[11]

> *For this reason the employer must make a reasonable effort to investigate the complaint honestly and impartially. This the defendant did. In my view, given the nature of the complaints and the need for the defendant to take action to protect both itself and the complainants, it did act fairly in adopting the course of action it did.*

BC does encourage employers to conduct an immediate investigation and attempt to remedy the unfair conduct. The approach in BC is designed to reward the employer for such action by allowing for a dismissal of the complaint. See *McLuckie v. London Drugs and another* for an example of such a decision.[12]

BC requires an employer to make a meaningful investigation of an apparent human rights violation. In *Bertrend v. Golder Associates*,[13] the employer's decision to terminate the probationary employment of the complainant was found to be a Code violation as it failed to take steps to investigate her behaviour which reflected an emotional issue:

> *Ms. Bertrend's depression does not insulate her from termination. However, once she disclosed her depression and raised an allegation of discriminatory conduct in the context of an employment offer, Golder had a responsibility to investigate Ms. Bertrend's complaint. It had communicated that commitment to its employees under its harassment policy.*

The Nova Scotia Board of Inquiry in *Cromwell v. Leon's Furniture Limited*[14] clearly concluded that the employer had an obligation to make an appropriate investigation and failed to do so. It, however, did not make an independent damage award due to this finding.

There are no cases offering an independent award for failure to investigate a complaint in other jurisdictions.

11 *Kinch v. Amoco,* 1998, accessed September 2014.
    http://www.canlii.org/en/ab/abqb/doc/1998/1998abqb171/1998abqb171.html
12 *McLuckie v. London Drugs and another,* 2009, accessed September 2014.
    http://www.canlii.org/en/bc/bchrt/doc/2009/2009bchrt409/2009bchrt409.html
13 *Bertrend v. Golder Associates,* 2009, accessed September 2014.
    http://www.canlii.org/en/bc/bchrt/doc/2009/2009bchrt274/2009bchrt274.html
14 *Cromwell v. Leon's Furniture Limited,* 2014, accessed September 2014.
    http://www.canlii.org/en/ns/nshrc/doc/2014/2014canlii16399/2014canlii16399.html

10
Reprisals

Reprisal allows for a remedy even where the main claim may fail. If you accuse the company of demoting you because of your age and the company fires you because of this assertion, you have a reprisal claim. You can recover a damage claim even if you cannot prove that the demotion was due to your age.

1. Reprisal Claims for Each Province and Territory

All legislatures across Canada have a reprisal or retaliation provision which differ in wording from statute to statute, although the substantive impact is the same. The following sections discuss each province and territory and how it works in each jurisdiction.

1.1 Ontario

The general remedy for reprisal is found in section 8 of the Ontario Code which states:

> *Every person has a right to claim and enforce his or her rights under this Act, to institute and participate in proceedings under this Act, and to refuse to infringe a right of another person under this Act, without reprisal or threat of reprisal for so doing.*

The purpose of this provision is to allow complainants to be able to enforce their rights without the fear of repercussion. The Ontario Code has a general related provision entitled "infringement" which prevents an employer from doing anything which may infringe a right under the Code.

Unlike other human rights violations, the employee needs to prove the intent to retaliate for the filing of the complaint or the threatened filing of the complaint. As noted, the conduct in question must show a deliberate intent to retaliate and such intention must be shown to have violated the section 8 remedy. As stated in *Chan v. Tai Pan Vacations:*[1]

> *The intention of section 8 is to allow complainants to pursue their rights under the Code without fear of reprisal for doing so. It is established human rights law that reprisal must involve a deliberate intent to retaliate and thus this intention must be demonstrated in order to show that a complainant's rights under section 8 have been violated.*

In *Murchie v. JB's Mongolian Grill,*[2] the Tribunal found that reprisal was proven on the facts before it. Reprisal can be a response to a complainant for contacting the Commission or threatening to do so in Ontario and in most other jurisdictions.

You need to prove intent, but that intent need not be the sole cause of the retaliation, only an influence. To constitute reprisal, it is sufficient if the conduct is "at least in part" due to the complaint or threatened complaint:

> *[176] It is settled law that when a respondent's treatment of a complainant is at least in part reprisal for contacting the Commission or threatening to do so, that section 8 has been engaged ...*

> *[177] First, Ms. Murchie's keys and pass-code were taken from her, in part, because Ms. Conyers was suspicious that Ms. Murchie would take the management logs without permission. Ms. Conyers did not like Ms. Murchie's "demeanour." Because Mr. Odd was visibly upset, he was not under the same cloud of suspicion, during the investigation.*

1.2 British Columbia

The law in BC allows for a retaliation complaint to be made, but there is a requirement that the reprisal come from the actual filing of a complaint, as opposed to the threat of so doing. This makes no sense but such was the decision in *Cariboo Chevrolet Pontiac Buick GMC Ltd. v. Becker.*[3] One would expect that a reprisal taken as a consequence of a declared intent to commence a complaint would make the grade, but such is not the law in BC.

---

1   *Chan v. Tai Pan Vacations*, 2009, accessed September 2014.
     http://www.canlii.org/en/on/onhrt/doc/2009/2009hrto273/2009hrto273.html
2   *Murchie v JB's Mongolian Grill*, 2006, accessed September 2014.
     http://www.canlii.org/en/on/onhrt/doc/2006/2006hrto33/2006hrto33.html#_ftn1
3   *Cariboo Chevrolet Pontiac Buick GMC Ltd. v. Becker*, 2006, accessed September 2014.
     http://www.canlii.org/en/bc/bcsc/doc/2006/2006bcsc43/2006bcsc43.html

1.3 Alberta

The Alberta legislation allows for a reprisal claim in response to an actual complaint or an attempted complaint. Such a reprisal claim can be made on a behalf of a person who had given evidence in a hearing, or otherwise participated in a hearing, or has made disclosure in a proceeding under the statute or has in any way assisted a person in the making of a complaint. This wording is typical of many other Canadian human rights statutes.

1.4 Saskatchewan

Section 45 of the Saskatchewan Code forbids a reprisal due to the filing or threatened filing of a complaint, due to disclosure of evidence, testifying or likely testifying, or participation in any other way in a proceeding under the Act.

1.5 Manitoba

Manitoba has a very broad reprisal provision which covers the same grounds as that of Saskatchewan. It forbids a reprisal due to the filing or threatened filing of a complaint, due to disclosure of evidence, testifying or likely testifying, or participation in any other way in a proceeding under the Act. In addition, it provides protection to any person who has complied with a Code obligation or has refused to contravene the Code. For example, a manager who has refused to terminate an employee based on gender, and in turn is terminated for this reason, would have a remedy under the Manitoba statute.

1.6 Quebec

The Quebec Charter of Human Rights and Freedoms has a very broad protective provision which prohibits unlawful interference with any Charter right. If the action in question is intentional, punitive damages may be awarded; otherwise, the offended party may claim "compensation for the moral or material prejudice."

1.7 Nova Scotia

Nova Scotia's reprisal provision provides protection to a person who has threatened a complaint or filed a complaint. It also allows a remedy for adverse treatment afforded to a person who has given evidence or assistance given in the proceeding.

1.8 New Brunswick

New Brunswick's statute prohibits adverse treatment due to the making of a complaint, giving evidence, or assisting in any way the initiation of the complaint.

1.9 Newfoundland and Labrador

The legislation of Newfoundland and Labrador prohibits reprisal due to the making of a complaint, the giving of evidence, or helping in respect of the initiation or furtherance of a complaint.

1.10 Prince Edward Island

Prince Edward Island prevents adverse treatment due to the making of a complaint, giving evidence, or assisting with respect to the initiation of the case.

1.11 Yukon

The *Yukon Human Rights Act* is simple, effective, and to the point. It prohibits retaliatory action or a threat of same against any person who has done or proposes to do anything permitted by the Act.

1.12 Northwest Territories

The Northwest Territories statute forbids reprisal against a person who has made or has threatened to make a complaint, or given evidence or otherwise participated in a proceeding or has intended to so.

1.13 Nunavut

The Act of Nunavut allows for a remedy in favour of any person who has been treated adversely due to notifying the Tribunal of a complaint or attempting to do so, given evidence or indicated an intent to do so, or otherwise participated or assisted in a hearing under the Act.

1.14 Federal statute

The federal statute allows for a reprisal remedy on behalf of a person who has filed a complaint or for the alleged victim where there has been retaliation or threatened retaliation.

11
Preventive Action for Employers

The first step for any company is to develop an effective anti-discrimination policy and to ensure proper training be given to management and other employees. The policy should allow for an internal complaint procedure to permit an adversely treated employee to bring his or her concerns forward without the fear of reprisal. The same policy may also include anti-harassment terms or this may be in a separate document.

It must also clearly define what rights are protected under the human rights code with as much clarity as possible. It should state the company's commitment to human rights and to promote equality in the workplace. It should not just be a feel good document but should be used actively in day-today business.

It should also note its application to all employees, including volunteers and occasional workers. It should state that it offers its protections even where a person may not outwardly appear to be offended and has not vocally objected. It should also deal with the concept of a poisoned work environment and note the duty on management staff to take affirmative steps to eliminate offensive conduct.

Apart from satisfying the legal requirement to have such a policy, this may also have the impact of internalizing the complaint process and avoid third-party intervention by the filing of a formal complaint. Human rights boards are not over the moon to see that as an objective, but the reality is that a concern which is raised internally and the employee sees an active response and a good-faith attempt to analyze and fix a problem will likely help end the situation quickly.

A good example of a case in which the court was critical of the policy created by the employer and the failure to investigate the claim diligently is the Nova Scotia decision of *Cromwell v. Leon's Furniture Limited*.[1] This was so, even though the court agreed that the employer had invested considerable resources into the creation of the manual. It nonetheless failed to define what conduct was discriminatory and what conduct was harassment.

1. An Effective Investigation

Once the employer is aware of a complaint, there should be an effective investigation undertaken, preferably by impartial persons, as soon as possible.

In British Columbia, an immediate and effective investigation taken by the employer, followed by appropriate remedial steps may result in the dismissal of the complaint. A good example of this conduct is the case of *McLuckie v. London Drugs and another*.[2] The complainant had alleged a representative of the company made inappropriate comments about her sexual preference, made other alleged comments which she considered sexual, and also inappropriately touched her.

The company investigated the complaint and ordered that the alleged offender be assigned into a different department to avoid direct contact. This action was found to be fair and the complaint was dismissed. The Tribunal stated the reasons for dismissing the case:

> The Tribunal has determined that, in cases where the respondent has taken steps to address the alleged discriminatory conduct, it may not further the purposes of the Code to further process the complaint ... the Tribunal explained its reasoning:
>
> > A number of common threads can be discerned underlying these decisions. One has to do with efficiency and avoiding the duplication of resources: it may not further the purposes of the Code to proceed with a complaint where to do so would result in the unnecessary duplication of the Tribunal's or the parties' resources ... A third has to do with encouraging parties to comply with their obligations under the Code without recourse to the Tribunal: it may not further the purposes of the Code to proceed with a complaint where the underlying dispute has been settled ...

The policy document should also speak to the issue of accommodation and why accommodation may be required in certain circumstances, such as issues involving disability, family status, and child care or other family

---

1   *Cromwell v. Leon's Furniture Limited*, 2014, accessed September 2014.
    http://www.canlii.org/en/ns/nshrc/doc/2014/2014canlii16399/2014canlii16399.html#par323
2   *McLuckie v. London Drugs and another*, 2009, accessed September 2014.
    http://www.canlii.org/en/bc/bchrt/doc/2009/2009bchrt409/2009bchrt409.html

needs, religion, creed, or age. It should state that the making of an accommodation request will not be judged adversely against the person for the initiation of the request and that all such submissions will be acted on in good faith.

The employer should also take steps to train its management staff on issues of human rights and also to educate all staff members of the need for human rights compliance and to be aware of the mechanics of enforcing the manual.

I know that all this sounds onerous, particularly for a small business that must attend to the same issues as a multinational company, but the reality is that it must be done and actually will do wonders to foster a positive work environment and minimize employee turnover.

2. Canada Labour Code's Policy on Sexual Harassment

The Canada Labour Code speaks to the requirement of the employer to maintain a workplace free of harassment. Within Division XV.1 — Sexual Harassment, the federal Code states that "every employee is entitled to employment free of sexual harassment" (section 247.2).[3] It also requires the employer to "make every reasonable effort to ensure that no employee is subjected to sexual harassment" (section 247.3).

In addition, the employer must develop a "policy statement" with respect to sexual harassment which must include "a statement to the effect that every employee is entitled to employment free of sexual harassment" and "a statement to the effect that the employer will make every reasonable effort to ensure that no employee is subjected to sexual harassment." The employer also must "make each person under the employer's direction aware of the policy statement" in section 247.4.

Prince Edward Island's *Employment Standards Act*, section 27 also requires a sexual harassment policy be in place.[4]

Ontario passed amendments to its *Occupational Health and Safety Act*,[5] which requires most employers to provide a harassment policy. This is not a human rights policy, but a harassment policy, or more appropriately, an anti-harassment policy. The failure to put one in place may be itself a breach of a fundamental term required by law. The amended sections provide, in part for the following:

Policies, violence and harassment

32.0.1 (1) An employer shall,

(a) prepare a policy with respect to workplace violence;

---

3   Canada Labour Code, 1985, sections 247.2 and 247.3, accessed September 2014.
      http://www.canlii.org/en/ca/laws/stat/rsc-1985-c-l-2/latest/rsc-1985-c-l-2.html#sec247.2_smooth
4   *Employment Standards Act*, 1988, accessed September 2014.
      http://www.canlii.org/en/pe/laws/stat/rspei-1988-c-e-6.2/latest/rspei-1988-c-e-6.2.html
5   *Occupational Health and Safety Act*, 1990, accessed September 2014.
      http://www.canlii.org/en/on/laws/stat/rso-1990-c-o1/latest/rso-1990-c-o1.html

(b' ... *ct to workplace harassment; and*

... *is necessary, but at least annu-*

Wr...

(2) *Th...* ... *and shall be posted at a*
    cons... ... *99, c. 23, s. 3.*

Exception

(3) *Subsectio...* ... *of workers regu-*
    larly emplo... ... *er, unless an in-*
    spector order... ... *, 2011, c. 1, Sched. 7,*
    s. 2 (3).

A similar provision exists ... *ccupational Health and Safety Act* of Saskatchewan which cove... ...e than human rights abuse, as is the case in Ontario.

The British Columbia workers' compensation legislation[6] also allows for a complaint of bullying or harassment and requires a policy be in place. Manitoba requires the same.

---

6 *Workers Compensation Act*, Work Safe BC, accessed September 2014. http://www2.worksafebc.com/ Publications/OHSRegulation/GuidelinesWorkersCompensationAct.asp#SectionNumber:G-D3-115_1-3

12
Tips for the Employers: Defending the Case

The employer can defend the case by leading evidence to show what the true motivation and reason for its actions was, and rebut the charge of adverse treatment. For example, if an applicant asserts that he was not hired due to his race and offers statistical or other evidence to support the inference, the employer can reply by leading evidence to show that the education and background experience of the complainant was lacking, which was the reason for the decision.

The same concept applies to any liability defence. The employer should show evidence to demonstrate what the apparent motivator was, as opposed to simply denying the alleged offensive action.

In a case involving a medical disability, or any case requiring accommodation, such as creed and family status, the test of "undue hardship" is a difficult one to meet, but it can be done. The test includes a procedural aspect that requires the employer to show what steps it took to determine the nature of the relevant issue and then assess how it might be able to accommodate the request. External advice may be required. The employee must cooperate in this endeavour. Disability cases will require the employee to be cooperative and share details of the nature of the restrictions, whether the condition is temporary or permanent.

The employer must then lead evidence to show why it could not offer accommodation. This requires proof of the nature of hardship, the expense, the difficulty this presented, and the impact on the business. The consequences of such accommodation on other employees is also a factor to be considered.

At all times, the employer should also be prepared to show that it quickly and diligently investigated the merits of the complaint as soon as it was made aware of the issue. This is important not only because it is required to do so, but also because it will have access to timely evidence which it can use to defend itself, as may be appropriate.

The employer policy manual may be of assistance as well in the early stages. It will encourage any alleged victims to come forward freely and also tend to internalize the issue and minimize the likelihood of litigation.

Sexual harassment claims are particularly difficult as the employer often has no view of which party is correct in the allegation or the denial. A third-party investigator can be useful at this stage to try to make factual findings of what actually did happen. This report will not be binding on a human rights tribunal but it can give the employer some direction as to what did happen. It may also be influential in leading to a resolution or putting into place remedial steps which may avoid litigation.

In Ontario, the employer is not deemed liable for the sexually offensive conduct of its employees, provided that the actions are not those of the directing mind of the company.

Not all sexual harassment cases are considered equal. Some can be very serious and some may involve conduct which is offensive, yet not worthy of termination if the offending employee is to be reprimanded. Similarly, if there has been a finding of improper conduct, it does not necessarily follow that the aggrieved employee may argue that he or she may cease employment due to a poisoned work environment and claim an income loss. There must be a contextual review of the conduct to determine where on the spectrum the offence may lie.

1. Lost Income Awards

As discussed in Chapter 8, for a lost income award, even if there is a finding of fault, there is no necessity that the award for lost income be set for the time period to the date of hearing, as many cases have done. The employer may show evidence that even if the complainant was not terminated, the person's employment would have terminated for other reasons unconnected to a human rights issue. For example, if the company suffered a loss of business and had made plans to reduce its workforce, which would inevitably have led to the termination of the complainant, the claim for lost income would come to an end at a certain date.

Similarly any other legitimate business reason, apart from a loss of business, which would have caused the complainant even a risk to being terminated, may factor into the calculation of the income loss.

If the employee had shown serious performance issues prior to termination, even if there is a finding of adverse treatment that led to the termination, the employer may still argue that the likelihood of long-term employment was remote and the claim for lost income should be abridged. The theory of this determination of the claim for lost income is based on the obligation of the claimant to prove a causal link between the adverse conduct of the employer and the claim for lost income. The Alberta Court of Appeal in *Walsh v. Mobil Oil Canada* (referenced in earlier chapters) stated that "there must be a causal link between the discriminatory practice and the loss claimed."

The test becomes: But for the employer's adverse conduct, what income would have the applicant otherwise have received? This allows the employer to introduce evidence to prove that even if there was no termination for adverse reasons, the employee would have been legitimately terminated for other business reasons.

The employer may also argue that the complainant has not taken reasonable steps to seek other employment. This is a tough case as the company must not only show that the employee was not diligent in his or her job search, but also that if he or she did so, such attempts would likely have been successful. This means calling evidence from another employer to confirm that this company would have likely hired him or her had there been an application. This may be an awkward and formidable task, which may be the reason that this defence rarely yields results.

2. Reinstatement

As discussed in more detail in Chapter 7, the reinstatement remedy is not reflexive and is within the discretion of the decision maker. Often the employee does not seek reinstatement. Where it is requested, the employer may offer evidence as to why a continued relationship of employment is unworkable. The list of reasons may be infinite. It may include the inherent difficulty in dealing with a person who has litigated with the employer, personal relationships within the company, a decline in the size of the workforce, loss of business, the likelihood of there being an unproductive working environment, and any other factors showing prejudice to the employer in the making of this order.

Care should be taken in making this submission as a denial of reinstatement, where the employee remains unemployed, could lead to a future income loss beyond the date of hearing.

3. Settlement Offers

It may be a difficult pill to swallow but sometimes the employer's best defence may be to admit the error. Where the complainant's case seems to be valid, an offer from the employer to pay reasonable damages for hurt feelings, a fair income loss, and even an offer of re-employment, particularly when made early on, may be the best defence.

Many complainants have no interest in returning to active employment. Even when such an offer is refused, this could be the company's best defence.

Legal costs are not awarded in Ontario to either party, successful or otherwise. Even in the jurisdictions which contemplate cost orders, these are generally reserved for exceptionally outrageous behaviour. Accordingly even a successful defence will represent an unrecovered cost, a factor to be considered in the interests of an early resolve.

Ontario, BC, and Nunavut are the only jurisdictions which employ the direct user access system. In every other jurisdiction, the human rights commission controls the process of the complaint. Apart from Quebec, in each of these provinces and territories, the commission has the ability to drop the case if it is of the view a reasonable offer of settlement has been made. There is a big advantage to take a reasonable approach where liability looks imminent and end the case, even without the claimant's consent, which can be done. Typically the commission is not interested in litigation where a reasonable settlement can be obtained.

In Quebec, the individual has the right to take the case to hearing where the commission decides to cease its involvement.

4. Motion to Dismiss

Because many claimants in BC and Ontario are unrepresented and there is no gatekeeper such as the human rights commission, as is the case in most of the remaining jurisdictions, motions to dismiss are relatively common and may be successful.

The test to show success on such a motion is set out in section 1. There are, again, two popular arguments:

- *Even if the claim is taken as valid and factual on the complaint that was filed, there is no violation of the code made.*

- *The evidence does not support a claim and there is no reasonable chance of success.*

- *The advantage of bringing such a motion is that the worst case for the employer is that the complainant will likely show all the evidence to support the case at an early stage. The best result, of course, would be an early dismissal.*

13
Workers' Compensation Defence

The case law has developed to allow a defence based on the relevant workers' compensation legislation where the following applies:

- *The statute allows for mental distress claims under the workers' compensation legislation.*

- *There has been a civil case commenced for emotional distress based on a workplace incident.*

Successful arguments have been made that jurisdictions which do not allow workers' compensation claims based on workplace mental distress are unconstitutional.

The impact of workers' compensation statutes on civil claims alleging emotional distress claims is nothing less than earth-shattering in the world of employment law. The bigger issue is whether this defence will apply to a human rights case, which seeks damages for emotional distress and/or lost income as a consequence of the emotional harm suffered. This means that the lost income claim must be connected to the emotional distress claim. For example, a woman asserts she has been treated abusively in the workplace due to gender and ceases work, alleging that the work environment is poisoned.

The leading case allowing the defence to a civil case is the March 2013 decision of *Ashraf v. SNC Lavalin ATP Inc.*,[1] which was upheld on appeal in November 2013.[2] The Court concluded that there could be no civil action for emotional distress damages due to workplace conduct, where the plaintiff was covered by workers' compensation legislation. "Accident" is defined in all such statutes across Canada to include intentional conduct.

Not all provinces allow for emotional distress claims under the workers' compensation legislation. The jurisdictions which do not allow workers' compensation claims for psychological damage are Manitoba, New Brunswick, Nova Scotia, and Northwest Territories. Ontario has a serious qualifier for such claims as does the amended statute in British Columbia to a certain extent.

Charter arguments have been successfully presented to challenge workers' compensation statutes which do not honour claims based on psychological suffering. Ontario's statute presently allows claims for psychological stress only where there has been an acute reaction to a sudden and unexpected traumatic event. The Ontario Act in 1997 defined the eligibility for a mental distress claim as follows:

> *13 ...*
>
> *(4) Except as provided in subsection (5), a worker is not entitled to benefits under the insurance plan for mental stress.*
>
> *(5) A worker is entitled to benefits for mental stress that is an acute reaction to a sudden and unexpected traumatic event arising out of and in the course of his or her employment. However, the worker is not entitled to benefits for mental stress caused by his or her employer's decisions or actions relating to the worker's employment, including a decision to change the work to be performed or the working conditions, to discipline the worker or to terminate the employment.*

This entitlement was further refined by a guidance statement known as "policy document 15-03-02," which acknowledges that persistent harassment will be covered where the most recent event has led to an acute psychological reaction. The application of the policy is made mandatory for the Appeals Tribunal by section 126(1) of the Act.

1. Charter Challenges to Workers' Compensation Legislation

The Nova Scotia legislation which prevented claims based on chronic pain was determined to be contrary to the Charter of Rights and Freedoms in the 2003 Supreme Court of Canada decision in *Nova Scotia (Workers'*

---

1 *Ashraf v. SNC Lavalin ATP Inc.*, 2013, accessed September 2014.
   http://www.canlii.org/en/ab/abqb/doc/2013/2013abqb143/2013abqb143.html
2 *Ashraf v. SNC Lavalin ATP Inc.*, 2013, accessed September 2014.
   http://www.canlii.org/en/ab/abqb/doc/2013/2013abqb688/2013abqb688.html

Compensation Board) v. Martin; Nova Scotia (Workers' Compensation Board) v. Laseur.[3]

A similar argument was made in *Plesner v. British Columbia Hydro and Power Authority*[4] before the British Columbia Court of Appeal in 2009. The British Columbia legislation contained words which were similar to the Ontario statute which limited the right of the claimant for benefits due to mental distress:

> *5.1(1) Subject to subsection (2), a worker is entitled to compensation for mental stress that does not result from an injury for which the worker is otherwise entitled to compensation, only if the mental stress*
>
> *(a) is an acute reaction to a sudden and unexpected traumatic event arising out of and in the course of the worker's employment,*
>
> *(b) is diagnosed by a physician or a psychologist as a mental or physical condition that is described in the most recent American Psychiatric Association's Diagnostic and Statistical Manual of Mental Disorders at the time of the diagnosis, and*
>
> *(c) is not caused by a decision of the worker's employer relating to the worker's employment, including a decision to change the work to be performed or the working conditions, to discipline the worker or to terminate the worker's employment.*

The majority of the Court determined the legislation to be contrary to the Charter and was determined to be of no force and effect.

BC passed amending legislation effective July 1, 2012, by *The Workers Compensation Amendment Act* 2011, S.B.C. 2012, c.23, to allow for workers' compensation claims due to a mental disorder which arises due to a reaction to traumatic events in the employment relationship or caused by bullying or harassment at work.

A similar challenge is in process in Ontario, which is presently before the Workers' Compensation Board. A human rights complaint has also been made by the employee, which has been deferred pending the decision of the Board.[5]

A recent decision of the Appeal Tribunal has stated that this limitation on mental distress claims under the Ontario workers' compensation statute is unconstitutional as it offends the equality section of the Charter. This will allow claimants with work-related mental distress claims entitlement to workers' compensation benefits. This consequence would deprive such persons of civil claims for emotional distress due to work-related trauma in industries covered by the Act.

---

3 *Nova Scotia (Workers' Compensation Board) v. Martin; Nova Scotia (Workers' Compensation Board) v. Laseur*, 2003, accessed September 2014. http://www.canlii.org/en/ca/scc/doc/2003/2003scc54/2003scc54.html

4 *Plesner v. British Columbia Hydro and Power Authority*, 2009, accessed September 2014. http://www.canlii.org/en/bc/bcca/doc/2009/2009bcca188/2009bcca188.html#par17

5 *Seberras v. Workplace Safety and Insurance Board*, 2012, accessed September 2014. http://www.canlii.org/en/on/onhrt/doc/2012/2012hrto1513/2012hrto1513.html

2. Workers' Compensation Statutes Can Affect Human Rights Claims

There remains a further argument that the workers' compensation statutes may deprive the relevant human rights commission of jurisdiction to award a damage claim for such a violation, given appropriate coverage. Generally, human rights legislation is considered quasi-constitutional and as such, supersedes any conflicting statute, unless specifically stated to the contrary in the human rights enabling legislation.

Apart from the quasi-constitutional status argument, the human rights process does deal with broader issues from a public interest perspective and includes other forms of non-monetary relief, including reinstatement, which is not available by a workers' compensation claim.

The recent acceptance of mental distress claims under workers' compensation statutes may deny or limit the right of the individual to use a human rights statute for compensatory damages or lost income.

The Supreme Court of Canada in its 1996 decision in *Béliveau St-Jacques v. Fédération des employeés et employés de services publics inc.*,[6] considered a similar issue where there was conflict between the workers' compensation statute and the Quebec Charter. The plaintiff had received compensation under the Quebec workers compensation legislation with the Commission de la santé de la sécurité du travail ("CSST") for "an employment injury" due to conduct of sexual harassment.

She had also commenced a civil action against the alleged harasser and her employer based on the same improper sexual advances under the remedy available through the Charter. The employer argued that due to waiver of civil remedy under the workers' compensation legislation that she was barred from civil action. The plaintiff's remedy in the civil claim was based on the Quebec Charter of Human Rights and Freedoms which provided as follows:

> *49. Any unlawful interference with any right or freedom recognized by this Charter entitles the victim to obtain the cessation of such interference and compensation for the moral or material prejudice resulting therefrom.*

> *In case of unlawful and intentional interference, the tribunal may, in addition, condemn the person guilty of it to exemplary damages.*

> *51. The Charter shall not be so interpreted as to extend, limit or amend the scope of a provision of law except to the extent provided in section 52.*

> *52. No provision of any Act, even subsequent to the Charter, may derogate from sections 1 to 38, except so far as provided by those sections, unless such Act expressly states that it applies despite the Charter.*

6 Béliveau St-Jacques v. Fédération des employées et employés de services publics inc., 1996, accessed September 2014. http://www.canlii.org/en/ca/scc/doc/1996/1996canlii208/1996canlii208.html

The Quebec Charter specifically allowed for an award of exemplary or punitive damages. It was noted by the court that the Charter maintained a special status of a quasi-constitutional substance:

> Like the statutes that are its counterparts in the other provinces, the Charter, which was enacted in 1975, has a special quasi constitutional status. Certain of its provisions thus have relative primacy, resulting from s. 52. By its very nature, such a statute calls for a large and liberal interpretation that allows its objectives to be achieved as far as possible. In this sense, not only the provisions at issue but the entire statute must be examined ... In Quebec, s. 53 indeed provides that if any doubt as to interpretation arises, it must be resolved in keeping with the intent of the Charter.

However, Gonthier J., writing for the majority of the Supreme Court of Canada determined that there was no remedy available under the Charter:

> I am therefore of the view that s. 438 has the effect of validly barring the victim of an employment injury from bringing an action for damages under the Charter. By making this exclusion, the AIAOD clearly does not violate any of the rights guaranteed in ss. 1 to 38 of the Charter. Moreover, victims of employment injuries are not denied all forms of monetary compensation. Rather, they are subjected to a special scheme, which offers a number of advantages but which allows them to obtain only partial, fixed sum compensation. In this sense, and although the point is not determinative, it is worth noting that this Court has already held that a similar ban on civil liability actions by victims of work accidents did not violate s. 15 of the Canadian Charter of Rights and Freedoms (Reference re Workers' Compensation Act, 1983 (Nfld.), 1989 CanLII 86 (SCC), [1989] 1 S.C.R. 922).

The majority opinion did also refer to the right of the individual to file a grievance under a collective agreement and offered these words, which were not law but rather an indicator of the court's views, and nonetheless instructive of a view of the remedy of reinstatement and public interest remedies by analogy under the Human Rights Code:

> I shall therefore refrain from determining whether a grievance could have been filed in the instant case. If that had been the case, however, it is understood that the arbitrator could not have awarded damages for the prejudice suffered as a result of the employment injury. The exclusion of a civil liability action also applies to the grievance arbitrator. This being said, it is not inconceivable that an arbitrator dealing with such a grievance in these circumstances could have ordered other remedial measures, such as reinstatement or reassignment, if the collective agreement so allowed.

The Court appeared to allow for a reinstatement or public interest award and yet denied the right to seek a remedy for punitive or other damages.

Ontario's human rights legislation offers remedies not contemplated by the workers' compensation process, including reinstatement and perhaps more importantly, a public interest perspective, an issue which may distinguish the human rights process from a civil claim under the Quebec Charter.

The *Workplace Safety and Insurance Act* (WSIA) also denies the person seeking such relief the right to claim "all rights of action (statutory or otherwise)," which presumably will be argued to include the right to make a human rights complaint.

s.26 Benefits in lieu of rights of action

(2) **Entitlement to benefits under the insurance plan is in lieu of all rights of action (statutory or otherwise)** *that a worker, a worker's survivor or a worker's spouse, child or dependant has or may have against the worker's employer or an executive officer of the employer for or by reason of an accident happening to the worker or an occupational disease contracted by the worker while in the employment of the employer. 1997, c. 16, Sched. A, s. 26 (2); 1999, c. 6, s. 67 (6); 2005, c. 5, s. 73 (6). (emphasis added — ed.)*

The success of this argument would mean that the Tribunal would be deprived of jurisdiction, no doubt a significant conclusion. Given the argument that the WSIA is offside the Charter due to its restrictive recognition of emotionally related disabilities, this issue is one of paramount concern.

It would also be open for the employer to argue that the employee's remedy for a workplace human rights complaint alleging a mental distress claim and a lost income claim due to the emotional distress mandates a workers' compensation claim. The public interest component and perhaps even reinstatement could be left to the human rights tribunal.

All this is idle speculation. It nonetheless presents an employer, given workers' compensation entitlement in place, to a very interesting submission, one which will likely enter final debate in the Supreme Court of Canada some years from now.

3. Charter of Rights and Freedoms

The Charter of Rights and Freedoms does set out certain rights which are determined as rights of all persons. Section 15 of the Charter offers its protection to race, national or ethnic origin, colour, religion, sex, age, and disability (i.e., mental or physical).

The Charter does not create a right of action, unless there is a government actor. Statutes of all jurisdictions must comply with fundamental charter rights and values and can be struck down as unconstitutional should such a law be found to be in violation of a Charter value. For example, Ontario's legislation, which provided social and medical assistance to those suffering from a disability, denied its benefits to those persons suffering from alcoholism or drug addiction. This provision was determined to be contrary to the Charter of Rights and Freedoms by the Divisional Court, as confirmed by the Court of Appeal in the 2010 decision of *Ontario (Disability Support Program) v. Tranchemontagne.*[7]

As noted in Chapter 13, Ontario's workers' compensation law and that of Nova Scotia and BC were determined to be offside the Charter as each statute unfairly differentiated claims based on mental and physical injuries.

7 *Ontario (Disability Support Program) v. Tranchemontagne,* 2010, accessed September 2014. http://www.canlii.org/en/on/onca/doc/2010/2010onca593/2010onca593.html

14
Tax Considerations

The good news is that a payment for personal anguish will be considered non-taxable, as will a payment for the loss of future earnings. Likely, the same treatment will be given to a payment made in exchange for giving up the right of reinstatement.

You should be aware of these issues when negotiating a settlement of the claim. No one is suggesting that you do anything improper, but a payment for lost income will be taxable. Keep in mind when writing to suggest a settlement, these letters may be later required by the Canada Revenue Agency (CRA) to be produced if there is an audit.

A normal severance payment obtained through a common-law wrongful dismissal action will be considered taxable income. A payment made as damages for a human rights violation will be seen as non-taxable.

The *Income Tax Act* has created a definition of a payment defined as a "retiring allowance" which requires tax be paid on such sum:

> *The term is defined in subsection 248(1) of the Act as follows: "retiring allowance" means an amount ... received*
>
> *(b) in respect of a loss of an office or employment of a taxpayer, whether or not received as, on account or in lieu of payment of, damages or pursuant to an order or*

judgment of a competent tribunal, by the taxpayer ...

Section 56(1)(a)(ii) requires such sum be included as taxable income.

The issue then becomes what types of payments, if any, may be received that are similar but distinct from a "retiring allowance," which may be considered as non-taxable receipts outside the definition as above.

The CRA has recognized that payments made as compensation for a human rights violation will be a non-taxable payment. The relevant bulletin's key sections are reproduced below (CRA's "Retiring Allowances").[1]

CRA agrees that a termination payment may consist of several components, one of which may be taxable as a normal retiring allowance and others which may be considered non-taxable. The examples given in the bulletin of non-taxable payments include human rights violations and defamation claims, but the list also includes other tort claims such as negligent misrepresentation, aggravated or moral damages in the context of abusive conduct in a wrongful dismissal claim and also punitive damages. Paragraph 9 of the Bulletin states that the determination of the relevant components is a question of fact:

Types of Receipts

Damages

> *9. Generally, compensation received by an individual from the individual's employer or former employer on account of damages may be employment income, a retiring allowance, non-taxable damages, or a combination thereof. Such a determination is a question of fact, which requires a review of all relevant facts and documentation of each particular case.*

Section 12 of the bulletin contemplates personal injuries which were sustained before or after the loss of employment will be non-taxable receipts. The wording "before or after" may be significant as the language appears deliberately to omit injuries sustained at the time of termination. The claim made by the employee should be careful to make such a distinction. This would appear to relate to personal injuries which are distinct to those suffered due to a human rights violation:

> *12. Where personal injuries have been sustained before or after the loss of employment (for example, in situations of harassment during employment, or defamation after dismissal), the general damages received in respect of these injuries may be viewed as unrelated to the loss of employment and therefore non-taxable. In order to claim that damages received upon loss of employment are for personal injuries unrelated to the loss of employment, it must be clearly demonstrated that the damages relate to events or actions separate from the loss of employment. In making such a determination, the amount of severance that the employee would reasonably be entitled to will be taken into consideration.*

---

1   Interpretation Bulletin IT-337R4 "Retiring Allowances," Canada Revenue Agency, February 1, 2006, accessed September 2014. http://www.cra-arc.gc.ca/E/pub/tp/it337r4-consolid/it337r4-consolid-e.html

Human rights violations are treated separately, presumably because such claims often arise from the very fact of termination and are not distinguishable in time. Section 12 continues:

> *Similarly, general damages relating to human rights violations can be considered unrelated to a loss of employment, despite the fact that the loss of employment is often a direct result of a human rights violations complaint. If a human rights tribunal awards a taxpayer an amount for general damages, the amount is normally not required to be included in income. When a loss of employment involves a human rights violation and is settled out of court, a reasonable amount in respect of general damages can be excluded from income. The determination of what is reasonable is influenced by the maximum amount that can be awarded under the applicable human rights legislation and the evidence presented in the case. Any excess will be taxed as a retiring allowance.*

Ontario legislation contains no maximum sum set by statute. That being said, it is notable that the damages awards under the Code do tend to "cluster around $25,000," apart from any lost income or a reprisal award.

Civil actions for wrongful dismissal in Ontario may also contain a damage claim for human rights violations. Lawyers negotiating a fair compromise will look to awards of damages awarded by the Human Rights Tribunal and by trial judges, for a fair background of reasonable expectation.

There can be a variety of civil causes of action to allow for damage claims due to sexual harassment. Many of these cases have dramatically exceeded the damage sums awarded by the Tribunal under the Code and some have also awarded a prospective lost income claim and punitive damages. These claims will also be non-taxable, apart from any direct claim for historical loss of income.

The parties will be expected to set out clearly in settlement documentation the sum that has been attributed to non-taxable components and be prepared to rationalize the allocation, if called on to do so. The onus rests on the taxpayer to show that the settlement of the non-taxable sum was a "claim as existing apart from the loss of employment" as was the issue in *Fawkes v. The Queen*,[2] at paragraph 24, which dealt with an assertion that the severance sum paid was higher than that which would be normally expected in view of the alleged human rights violation asserting reinstatement and "ambiguous additional damages."

In *Dunphy v. The Queen*[3] the minutes did not allocate a specific sum to the alleged human rights violation, but the Federal Court nonetheless accepted that a bona fide claim was asserted and made an apportionment on its own assessment, splitting the respective positions.

In one case, the appellant taxpayer had failed in his request for all allocation of the settlement funds paid to him that were attributable to

---

2   *Fawkes v. The Queen*, 2004, accessed September 2014.
    http://www.canlii.org/en/ca/tcc/doc/2004/2004tcc653/2004tcc653.html
3   *Dunphy v. The Queen*, 2009, accessed September 2014.
    http://www.canlii.org/en/ca/tcc/doc/2009/2009tcc619/2009tcc619.html

a claim for harassment made against the employer. The settlement sum did not contain any allocation of the sum paid which was approximately $150,000. The Federal Court of Appeal concluded that the taxpayer had an obligation to produce "some evidence" to identify that the settlement did include non-taxable components:

> In the present matter, the Tax Court judge found that the appellant's evidence did not enable him to "clearly" determine this apportionment ... In saying this, the Tax Court judge, in my view, set the bar too high. As the Supreme Court explains, the evidence should be examined to see whether there is some evidence on which the judge can identify which part of the amount relates to each of the purposes referred to in the settlement.

The Court found such evidence in the form of the severance policy manual of the employer to determine the expected normal entitlement and concluded the balance should be allocated to the non-taxable harassment damages.

1. Some Claims Are Taxable

Not all claims recoverable under human rights legislation will be considered non-taxable. Lost income claims based on pay equity violations by virtue of the *Canadian Human Rights Act* have been held to be taxable as was the Federal Court decision in *Van Elslande v. The Queen*.[4]

Similarly, it would be expected that claims for historical lost income and not emotional distress in a sexual harassment claim would be considered taxable. It is to be noted that the IT Bulletin mentioned earlier in this chapter speaks of an award of "general damages." Care should be taken to distinguish a specific past lost income award and other damage claims arising from a human rights claim.

---

4   *Van Elslande v. The Queen*, 2007, accessed September 2014.
    http://www.canlii.org/en/ca/tcc/doc/2007/2007tcc370/2007tcc370.html

Resources

Website links often expire or web pages move, at the time of this book's publication these links were current.

CanLii

This is a free public access database of precedent cases with full search functions.

www.canlii.ca

Canadian Human Rights Act

http://www.canlii.org/en/ca/laws/stat/rsc-1985-c-h-6/latest/
rsc-1985-c-h-6.html

Canadian Human Rights Commission

http://www.chrc-ccdp.ca/eng

Alberta

Alberta Human Rights Act

http://www.canlii.org/en/ab/laws/stat/rsa-2000-c-a-25.5/latest/
rsa-2000-c-a-25.5.html

Alberta Human Rights Commission

> http://www.albertahumanrights.ab.ca/

British Columbia

BC Human Rights Code

> http://www.canlii.org/en/bc/laws/stat/rsbc-1996-c-210/latest/
> rsbc-1996-c-210.html

BC Human Rights Tribunal

> http://www.bchrt.bc.ca/

BC Human Rights Coalition

> http://www.bchrcoalition.org/

Manitoba

Manitoba Human Rights Code

> http://www.canlii.org/en/mb/laws/stat/ccsm-c-h175/latest/
> ccsm-c-h175.html

Manitoba Human Rights Commission

> http://www.manitobahumanrights.ca/

New Brunswick

New Brunswick Human Rights Act

> http://www.canlii.org/en/nb/laws/stat/rsnb-2011-c-171/latest/
> rsnb-2011-c-171.html

New Brunswick Human Rights Commission

> http://www.gnb.ca/hrc-cdp/index-e.asp

Newfoundland

Newfoundland and Labrador Human Rights Act

> http://www.canlii.org/en/nl/laws/stat/snl-2010-c-h-13.1/
> latest/snl-2010-c-h-13.1.html

Newfoundland and Labrador Human Rights Commission

> http://www.justice.gov.nl.ca/hrc/index.html

Northwest Territories

Northwest Territories Human Rights Act

> http://www.canlii.org/en/nt/laws/stat/snwt-2002-c-18/latest/
> snwt-2002-c-18.html

Northwest Territories Human Rights Commission

> http://nwthumanrights.ca/

Nova Scotia

Nova Scotia Human Rights Act

> http://www.canlii.org/en/ns/laws/stat/rsns-1989-c-214/latest/rsns-1989-c-214.html

Nova Scotia Human Rights Commission

> http://humanrights.gov.ns.ca/

Nunavut

Nunavut Human Rights Act

> http://www.canlii.org/en/nu/laws/stat/snu-2003-c-12/latest/snu-2003-c-12.html

Nunavut Human Rights Tribunal

> http://www.canlii.org/en/nu/laws/stat/snu-2003-c-12/latest/snu-2003-c-12.html

Ontario

Ontario Human Rights Code

> http://www.canlii.org/en/on/laws/stat/rso-1990-c-h19/latest/rso-1990-c-h19.html

The Human Rights Tribunal of Ontario

> http://www.hrto.ca/hrto/

Ontario Human Rights Commission

> http://www.ohrc.on.ca/en

Prince Edward Island

PEI Human Rights Act

> http://www.canlii.org/en/pe/laws/stat/rspei-1988-c-h-12/latest/rspei-1988-c-h-12.html

PEI Human Rights Commission

> http://www.gov.pe.ca/humanrights/

Quebec

Quebec Charter of Human Rights and Freedoms

> http://www.canlii.org/en/qc/laws/stat/cqlr-c-c-12/latest/cqlr-c-c-12.html

Quebec Human Rights Commission

> http://www.cdpdj.qc.ca/en/Pages/default.aspx

Saskatchewan

Saskatchewan Human Rights Code

http://www.canlii.org/en/sk/laws/stat/ss-1979-c-s-24.1/latest/ss-1979-c-s-24.1.html

Saskatchewan Human Rights Commission

http://saskatchewanhumanrights.ca/

Yukon

Yukon Human Rights Act

http://www.canlii.org/en/yk/laws/stat/rsy-2002-c-116/latest/rsy-2002-c-116.html

Yukon Human Rights Commission

http://www.yhrc.yk.ca/

OTHER TITLES OF INTEREST FROM SELF-COUNSEL PRESS

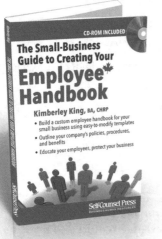

The Small Business Guide to Creating Your Employee Handbook

Kimberley King, BA, CHRP

ISBN 978-1-77040-201-0

6 x 9 • paper + CD-ROM • 80 pp.

First Edition

$14.95 CAD

What all great companies have in common is a well-defined set of rules recorded in an easily accessible employee handbook. *The Small-Business Guide to Creating Your Employee Handbook* provides you with all the information to create rules and regulations for your employees to follow. New and current employees will appreciate the information you set out in your employee handbook. It not only provides your employees with company policies but also provides protection against unfair treatment, discrimination, and legal claims. Your handbook will be a valuable communication tool for your business and your employees. This step-by-step guide will help you define professional conduct, establish health and safety requirements, describe group and other benefits, and construct social media policies. It also provides information on how to make a non-disclosure agreement so employees cannot give information about your company to your competitors, while they are employed by you or after they leave. The CD included with this book contains easy-to-use forms to help you prepare your small business' very own employee handbook.

The Author

Kimberley King, BA, CHRP, began her more than decade-long career as a human resources generalist with an investment management company, before transitioning into human resources management with two of Canada's major retailers. She has drafted and helped compile HR handbooks and one-off policies for each company she has worked for; being aware of how effective a well drafted and communicated handbook is for company productivity, she put together this HR handbook for small businesses that donít have the time or know-how to draft one for themselves. King's goal is to help small businesses with their HR needs, starting with this book.

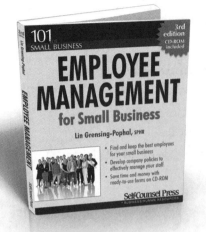

Employee Management for Small Business

Lin Grensing-Pophal, SPHR

ISBN: 978-1-55180-863-5

8¼ x 9¾ • paper + CD-ROM • 200 pp.

Third Edition

$23.95 CAD

Whether a business has 1 or 100 employees, *Employee Management for Small Business* provides the tools and knowledge required to take an active and positive approach to maintaining an effective human resources plan.

Finding and keeping good employees is crucial to the success of every business, but it s not easy. This book will show small-business owners how to develop a human resources plan tailored to their needs.

From hiring and orientation to developing company policies and negotiating employment contracts, this book covers the essentials of employee management.

Like all the books in the *101 for Small Business* series, each topic in the book is explained in simple language and is illustrated with real-world examples, checklists, and forms.

The Author

Lin Grensing-Pophal has written many business and employee management articles for general and trade publications, and is the author of several books published by Self-Counsel Press. She is accredited through the International Association of Business Communicators and the Society for Human Resource Management, and is a member of the American Society of Journalists and Authors.